THE

CHURCHYARD INSCRIPTIONS

OF THE

CITY OF LONDON.

TRANSCRIBED AND ABSTRACTED

BY

PERCY C. RUSHEN.

LONDON : PHILLIMORE & CO , LTD., 124 CHANCERY LANE.

1910

INTRODUCTION.

SOME years ago the writer was impressed with the rapid rate of disappearance of the externally situated memorial inscriptions in the City of London to its dead citizens. This has been due to two main causes, viz. · the action of the atmospheric elements and the sacrilegists who, while believing themselves Christians, think that, by statute, consecration may be undone and that that which has been dedicated to God may well be allocated to the mundane purposes of street widening and office building. On the whole the latter cause has effected the greater destruction, for it must be remembered that the custom of erecting memorials over the graves of the dead, when buried outside the church, is of comparatively recent favour, and the sordid tampering with consecrated ground has taken place in this city rather extensively from time to time since the custom referred to has been favoured. However, at the time the writer's mind was moved on the subject, the greater destructive influence was that of atmospheric conditions, for in recent years very few street alterations, etc, necessitating obliteration of consecrated ground have been carried out, and in the absence of this, public feeling has of late been strongly inclined to retention of all open spaces for hygienic reasons. The latter has, in fact, been carried to such an extent that in many cases the ground has been laid out for public use as gardens and places of public recreation, peaceful perhaps, but unfortunately too often used by the dirty loafer and those that work not. Nevertheless, the antiquary should be thankful for this public feeling, because, although, in many cases, in furtherance of the conversion, burial memorials, in the absence of special control by relatives of those commemorated, have had to be subservient to the exigencies of horticulture, yet the memorials have not been destroyed. The atmosphere of such a large city as London is naturally heavily charged with the emanations of civilisation, such as coal combustion products, comprising acidulous matter peculiarly destructive of materials such as limestone and marble, of which most burial memorials are made in the South of England. To such an extent is this destructive influence apparent that after the dry spring and summer of 1899, during which acidulous matter was deposited upon all the buildings of our city, the writer observed, during the first heavy autumnal storm of that year, the frothy ebullition upon the limestone walls of a city church due to the action of the diluted acid upon the carbonate of lime of the structure. Impressed with these considerations, and having a feeling of veneration and affection towards those worthy citizens lying in their narrow beds amidst all the sordid bustle and scenes they probably loved so well, the writer felt that it was a task worthy of his labour to turn " Old Mortality " for the time and faithfully record these fast disappearing memorials. The task was far greater than he imagined, but having entered upon it, he continued it to completion, taking care to transcribe every word and cipher possible, sparing neither patience nor soiling of hands and clothes in the work. Every transcript was made line for line, and even the style of lettering was copied in nearly all cases.

It was that found even at that time there still remained memorial inscriptions to the dead in no less than fifty-nine open spaces within the City, a few of the spaces really comprising burial grounds belonging to more than one parish. The majority of these grounds were closed to the general public and some had evidently only been entered at rare intervals. This exclusiveness had evidently, as well it might, disheartened well intentioned antiquaries in the past from doing the work that ought to have been carried out sixty years ago. It was undoubtedly the cause of more than half the labour and personal inconvenience expended and experienced by the writer in his task, entailing much correspondence, great delays and many attendances, although he acknowledges with pleasure the great courtesy that he generally experienced at the hands of incumbents and parochial officers. Destructive influences in the past had also been so great that the number of legible inscriptions was much less than the number of burial grounds in which they were distributed would lead one to suppose, and evidently in very small proportion to those existing when the grounds were closed for burials. After weeks of correspondence, in order to ascertain the officer who could give the copyist admittance to a little ground, it was found, perhaps, that there were but two inscriptions existing in it.

Although in the absence of help which is not forthcoming it is not possible to publish the complete transcripts of the epitaphs of the dead citizens of the greatest city of the world, yet it is found practicable to print abstracts of all of them, as is done in the following pages. These abstracts comprising, as they do, all facts stated in the inscriptions of any use to the genealogist, will, it is believed, be found very useful by him and by the antiquary generally. Moreover, the abstracts should be of interest to the citizen, and he is not uncommon, who even in these days of speed and suburban domicile is inclined to linger over the memories of those who in the past have helped to make our City what it is and who lived their life, experienced their joys and sorrows and died amidst the scenes that many City men now only couple with caretakers and ledgers. It may by some be considered morbid to linger on the memories of the dead or to live in the past at all, but it is not so. Mental journeys of this kind have a refining and civilizing influence as is proved by the fact that never at any time heretofore has the desire for identification and knowledge of particular ancestors, that is the study of genealogy, been stronger than it is to-day, when physically every thing appears superficially to be for future. The truth is that the mind, particularly that of high development, loves to dwell on the past at times—its joys are gilded and its sorrows whitened. It is the unknown future that appals. These feelings permeate all society, and the writer was once publicly and spontaneously thanked by a "labouring" man for transcribing burial inscriptions.

Since the writer's transcripts were made, many of the inscriptions have become illegible, or have disappeared, so that at the present time it is impossible to do the same work. The writer only regrets that he was not able to transcribe the inscriptions many years earlier, say at the time the City burial grounds were closed, about sixty years ago.

A curious instance of how conditions counteract automatically is afforded by the changes in the City. Prior to 1852, the population was so close that it was decided that City burial grounds should be closed to burials for hygienic reasons, and statutory provision was made accordingly, whereas in a very few years the density of population brought about its own remedy, for the area became too valuable for residential purposes. At the present time the resident population of the City is so much smaller that the old burial grounds would be ample burial accommodation without producing conditions any more unwholesome than those brought about by the vast cemeteries to which burials were transferred.

Those inquirers who are not well acquainted with London, must bear in mind that the City proper, being the locality covered by this work, forms now a very small portion of the great metropolis, although the most ancient, interesting and important portion To copy all the monumental inscriptions of London County would take almost a lifetime, and the writer must leave that task, not, he hopes, to a single labourer, but to many. He himself some years ago transcribed the greater number of those in Clerkenwell and Southwark

That monumental inscriptions afford valuable data to the genealogist, not ascertainable from Parish Registers, every student of such things knows. Relationships, ages, locality of origin, or residence, are frequently given, and to the inquirer constitute valuable links and guides to further search. Moreover such inscriptions constitute a good check to Parish Registers at times, for the occasional inconsistencies between the two records are not always due to errors on the memorials. In fact there are instances, although rare, of omission of burial entries in Registers when it is patent that the remains still rest in the burial ground of the parish

It may be noted that many of the Monumental Inscriptions which were externally situated when copied had originally been placed in the floors of the churches, but had been removed later to the outside elements to make room for the execrable pottery so much favoured for floors a few years ago This practice of removal cannot, in the writer's opinion, be too heartily condemned, for it immediately subjects to severe destructive agencies memorials that were never intended to be so exposed by the loving friends who inscribed the stones There is, notwithstanding the modern tendency to fear morbidity, nothing incongruous in the presence of memorials to the dead in buildings so closely connected with the mystery of human existence as places of worship.

The reader may discern occasionally in the following abstracts slight obscurities in statements of relationship, but these obscurities exist in the original inscriptions, for every care has been taken to make the abstracts exactly consistent with the originals

In conclusion the writer thanks all the clergy and other parish officers, too numerous to name, for their courtesy and trouble in affording facilities for making the transcripts.

PERCY C. RUSHEN.

10, WARWICK COURT,
  HIGH HOLBORN,
    LONDON, W.C.

CONTENTS.

Contents

The Churchyard Inscriptions of the City of London.

ST. ALBAN'S, WOOD STREET.
Ground around the Church.

Flat stone.

———— Busby, of the parish, died 22 May, 16—6, in his 44th year.

Placed by his relict SARAH BUSBY.

SAMUEL AARON died 26 January, 17—1, aged 70.

ALL HALLOWS, BARKING.
Ground around the Church.

Altar tombs

1. JOSEPH STEELE, late of Acrewalls, co. Cumb., and upwards of 70 years of this parish, died 30 September, 1835, in his 90th year.

    HENRY STEELE, his brother, whose remains were removed by faculty from St Andrew Undershaft Church and deposited here. Tomb restored in 1868 under a bequest for that purpose by the Baroness de Sternberg.

2. LYDIA, wife of SAMUEL DAVENPORT, of the parish, died 6 December, 1733, aged —.
    " Her children . . . blessed her."

Flat stones.

3. JONATHAN BARRAS, of the parish, died — January, 1747, aged 61.

    Also children by ANN, his wife, who died infants.

    JONATHAN BARRAS, his son, died ————, 1761, aged 33, also his infant children.

B

MARY, wife of last, died 27 September, 1766, aged 41.

ANN, wife of JONATHAN BARRAS, sen' died 8 April, 1776, aged 81.

4. Family grave of DANIEL and MARY JEWSON.

5. Family grave of J———— MORRICE.

Headstones.

6. Mrs. ANN CLOSS, only daughter of JOSEPH and SUSANNAH TURNLEY, late of the parish, died 13 April, 183—, aged 26.

SUSANNAH TURNLEY, died 30 August, 184—, aged 68.
> 51 years a wife

7. WILLIAM TUTCHING.

8. MARY, wife of JOB ELLIOT, of the parish, died 28 September, 1818, aged 43.

Four of their children who died infants.

JOB ELLIOT above, died 22 September, 1836, aged 59

ANN, their granddaughter, died 7 May, 184— aged 2

9. BRYANT WILLIAM ROBERTS, son of WILLIAM JAMES and MARY ROBERTS, born January —, died September —

10. WILLIAM CHRISTEY, of the parish, died 23 December, 1793, aged 70

ANN, his wife, died 17 April, 1802, aged 7—

ELIZABETH CHRISTEY, died 30 November, 1804, aged 3 year 6 months

WILLIAM CHRISTEY, died 1 December, 1804, aged 2 years 4 months
> Great grandchildren of above.

JOHN CHRISTEY, died 5 July, 1814, aged 45.
> Grandson of above.

WILLIAM ALEXANDER CHRISTEY, brother of last, died 2 November, 1826, aged 21.

CHARLES ALEXANDER CHRISTEY, son of WILLIAM & ANN CHRISTEY above, died 17 August, 1827, aged 66.

MARTHA, his wife died 12 January, 1829, aged 55.

11. Family grave of JAMES and JANE MARY MILLS of the parish. Their children —

GEORGE AUGUSTUS, died 9 March, 1802, aged 8 months

ANN, died 20 December, 1808, aged 1 year 8 months.

ELIZA, died 18 September, 1810, aged 2 years 10 months.

CHARLES FREDERICK, died 15 November, 1810, aged 1 year.

PRISCILLA ANN, died 25 September, 181 (5 or 3) aged 12 years 7 months.

SARAH MILLS, grandmother of above children, died 22 ————

JANE MARY MILLS, mother of above children and of 9 surviving died 14 October, 1831 ————

JAMES MILLS above, died [1 ?] July 184 [2 ?] aged 7—

12 ———— wife of WILLIAM POTTS, died — July, 17—, aged 45.

WILLIAM POTTS, of the parish, died 14 February, 1735, aged 47.

13. GEORGE STANER CARTER, son of JOHN and MARY CARTER, of the parish, died 11 February 18—, aged 2 years 7 months.

SARAH MATILDA CARTER, daughter of above, died 26 October, 1837, aged — months.

14. MRS. ANN MAYES, died 20 October, 1824, aged 63, for 19 years matron of the parish workhouse.

15 SARAH, wife of JOSEPH ROBINSON, of the parish, died 1 November, 1819, aged 70.

JOSEPH and MARY ROBINSON, grandchildren of above, died in infancy

JOSEPH ROBINSON died 8 August, 1831, aged 80

16. CATHERINE, wife of ————, late of Thames Street, died 22 July, 18—, aged 45.

Four of her children who died infants.

17 ANN, ELIZABETH, SAM, and THOMAS, sons and daughters of JOSEPH and MARY RUDGE, of Cable Street, who all died under 5 years of age.

WILLIAM BICKERTON, grandfather of above children, died 12 October, 1805, aged 67.

Mrs ANN BICKERTON, daughter of Major BICKERTON.

18. GRACE, wife of HENRY MUSSETT, of the parish, died 3 August, 1827, aged 35.

Five of their children died infants.

THOMAS MUSSETT, brother of above, died 22 November, 1835, aged 29

19. Children of WILLIAM and ANN RUSBY of the parish :—

LEONARD WILLIAM died 10 February, 1818, aged 7 days.

JAMES died 26 December, 1820, aged 18 months 14 days.

BRIDGET, died 11 May, 1826, 3 months 3 days.

WILLIAM RUSBY above died 31 March, 1848, aged 62.

20. JOHN DAVIS, late of Mansel Street, died 8 November, 182—, aged 79.

ANN WHALLY, daughter of above and wife of W. WHALLY, of the parish, died 24 October, 1834, in her 47th year.

Footstones

21. S.W., 1805. M.W., 1811. E.W., 1812. W.W., 1838.

22. J.T.B., 1823 E.—, 1826. J.—B., 1838

23. —T., 1774 M.R., 1780. —R. 1788. —, 179—. —A., 1813. J.A., 1823.

ALL HALLOWS-THE-GREAT.

Site of the Church which was demolished about 1895, and the ground around it

Flat stones.

1. ARMS — a spray of shamrock — on a chief — 3 estoiles or mullets of 6 points — for —
Vault of JAMES JACOBSON

2. Vault of JOHN TASH

3. RICHARD BENTLEY of the parish, died 23 February, 1808, aged 41

JAMES BENTLEY, his father, died 21 December, 1805, aged 64.

JOSEPH, brother to above RICHARD, died 15 ———
1806, aged —5.

——— BENTLEY ——————————— 1819.

4. THOMAS BROMLEY, Citizen and Soapmaker of
London, died 8 October, 1681, in his 69th year.

THOMAS, his son, died 7 March, 16—, in his 26th year.

HANNAH, his daughter, died — January, 1661, in
her 14th year.

SAMUEL, REBEKAH, and MARY his children, by
CATHERINE his wife, who all died in infancy.

ESTHER BROMLEY, grand-daughter of said THOMAS
and CATHERINE, died —2 November, 1677.

CATHERINE BROMLEY, wife of THOMAS, senr, died
23 February, 1687/8, aged 76.

NATHANIEL BROMLEY, son of NATHANIEL and ELIZA-
BETH BROMLEY, and Grandson to THOMAS, born
31 March, 1688, died 8 February, 169—

5. BRIDGET SHELBEY, sister to ELIZABETH WORREN,
died 19 October, 1700, aged 59.

JOHN WORREN, died 11(?) December, 1712, aged 66.

6. JOSEPH WHITE, of Dowgate Square, died 10 October,
1829, aged 51.

7. SUSANNA, wife of JAMES WRIGHT, of this parish,
died 6 March, 1809, aged 54.

ELIZABETH WRIGHT, their daughter, died 3 October,
1815, aged 34.

WILLIAM WRIGHT, their son, died 14 September,
1829, aged 38.

WILLIAM WRIGHT above, died 23 March, 1829, in
his 90th year.

8. THOMAS BRITTEN, died 10 November, 1821, in his
61st year.

ANNA, his relict, died 1— October, 1823, in her
52nd year.

9. Mrs. ELIZA DUMBLE died 5 July, 1835, aged 59.

10. MARTHA, wife of JOHN BICKERTON, died 9 November, 1757, aged 33.

SAMUEL, their son, died 8 November, 1763, aged
6 years 5 days.

Mrs. Elizabeth Bickerton, mother of the above John, died 10 June, 1774, aged 76.

Elizabeth, wife of Edward Chesterton, daughter of John and Martha Bickerton, died 31 March, 1779, in her 23rd year.

John Bickerton above, died 12 November, 1781, aged 60.

11 Elizabeth —— Bickerton, daughter of William and Elizabeth Bickerton, died — November, ——, aged 24

William Bickerton, died 15 March, 174—, aged 44.

William Bickerton, son —— died 13 May, 1774

12 Ezekiel Lewis, born 28 September, 1683, died 4 September, 1756

13 Robert Simpson, died 19 August, 1804, aged 11 months 14 days

John Simpson, of the parish, mason, his father, died 3 April, 180—, aged —2 years.

Elizabeth Simpson, his daughter, died 12 August, 1817, aged — years — months 6 days

Mary, his wife, died 1 (?) December, 1817, aged 76.

Most of the foregoing memorials were probably formerly in the floor of the Church

Headstones

14 Edward Willson, died 18 March, 1799, aged 48

Mary, his widow, died 20 March, 1821, aged 71

Mary Ann and Esther their children, who died infants.

15 Sarah Tudor, sister of Samuel Tudor, of the parish, died 10 August, 1833, aged 23.

Samuel, son of above Samuel, and Mary Heriot, his wife, died 26 July, 1828, aged 6 weeks

16. Samuel Clark, of the parish, died 12 December, 1790, aged 59.

Ann Clark, his widow, died 7 September, 1819, aged 79

Mrs. Frances Clark, late of St. Pancras parish, and daughter-in-law of above, died 9 October, 183—, aged 73

RICHARD CLARK, her husband, late of the Hon
East India Co 's service, and of Adelaide Place,
London Bridge, formerly of this parish, died
— May, 1844, in his 85th year

17.   MARY, wife of THOMAS TACK, of the parish, died
11 June, 1820, aged 47

THOMAS TACK above, died 16 May, 183[5?] aged 67.

THOMAS TACK his son, died 26 July, 183—, aged 41.

SARAH METHAM ———, mother of above MARY
TACK, buried 2— February, ——

ALL HALLOWS THE LESS

Site of the Church which was destroyed by the Great Fire
of 1666.

Altar tombs.

1.   Family vault of ALEXANDER NESBITT

2   Family vault of Mr. SHILLITO, 1834

3   " EDWARDS and MITFORD "

   Arms—1 Erm , a lion rampant [sa] for
       Edwardes.

     2. Arg., a fess sa between 3 [moles sa]
       2, and 1 for *Mitford*, of Mit-
       ford, impaling as shield 1
       above.

Mural tablet

4   WILLIAM JACKSON, merchant, died 8 December,
1792, aged 56.

Headstones

5.   Two young children of WILLIAM and ELIZABETH
PARKER of the parish

WILLIAM PARKER, their father, died 9 December,
1739, aged 63

WILLIAM PARKER, his son, died 1 December, 1739,
aged 20

ALICE GIBSON, daughter, died 20 November, 1749,
aged 3—

Mrs. ELIZABETH PARKER above died ————

6.   THOMAS PRATT, died 12 December, 1712, aged 55
ANN his wife.

7. Mrs. Rebecca Sims, died 19 March, 1747, aged 8—

   Mrs. Anna Sims, died suddenly 11 November, 1749, aged 60

   Joseph Sims, former husband of ————, died 23 July, 1750.

   Mary Sims, late wife of John Augustus Sims, died in childbed, 29 August, 1752, aged 21

   John Augustus Sims above.

8. Richard Green, died 12 January 1781 in his 87th year.

   Joseph, his son, died 7 December, 1761, aged 15

   Seven of his children died infants.

   Esther Green, wife of above Richard, died 19 November, 1796, in her 82nd year.

9. John Wall, of the parish, died —2 March, 1747, aged 4—.

   Two of his children who died young.

   Robert Barpi——, of the parish.

10. Elizabeth, wife of William Kentish, of the parish, died 2— October, 1717, aged 25, and her child

    James and Richard " by his present wife, Hannah Kentish."

11. John Longden, merchant of the parish, died 11 March, 1800, aged 41.

12. ————

    Also two of their children, Sarah died 6 December, 177—, aged 4 years 3 months.

    Lucy, died 23 December, 1774, aged 4 years 2 months

13. Mary, wife of Samuel Stretton, of the parish, died 20 March, 17—, aged 49.

    Also two children.

14. Ann, wife of ————d Meredith, died 20 October 1785, in her 50th year.

    Above ————d Meredith, died 31 Aug——

15. ———— Appleby.

16 OWEN JONES, died 26 September, 1814, aged 74
ROBERT ROBERTS, died 5 May, 1821, in his 64th year.
HANNAH JANE ROBERTS, widow of both above, died
23 April, 1838, aged 65

ALL HALLOWS, LOMBARD STREET.

Ground—South of the Church.

Flat stones

1 THOMAS BAYLI—, husband of ————, died 14
January ——, aged 69
Miss RUTH B————, died 25 June ————, aged 67,
2 THOMAS GREENH———, died 27 December, 1823,
aged 61.

ALL HALLOWS, STAINING

Site of the Church which was destroyed in the Great Fire of 1666.

Altar tomb

1 JANE MARY SHARPE, wife of Rev L. SHARPE,
Rector of the parish, died 3 June, 1823, aged 41.
Their children :—
MARY, died 30 May, 1814, aged 2
PHILIP, died in the East Indies, — February, 1824,
aged 15.
JAMES, died 6 February, 184—, aged 28.
ALEXANDER, died 2 — April, 1843, aged 30
Rev. LANCELOT SHARPE above, 30 years Rector of
the parish, died 26 October, 1851, in his
78th year.
CLARENCE HENRY, his son, by Mary, his wife, died
22 January, 18—, aged 2.
MARY, relict of L. SHARPE above, died 29 January,
1869, aged 80.

Flat stone

2. JOSEPH BARKER, formerly of the parish, late of St.

Leonard's, Shoreditch, died 11 December, 1845, aged 66 He bequeathed £150 for purchasing freedoms of William Winter's children of the parish.

Headstones

3　JOHN BARKER, died 16 October, 1796, aged 58
MARGARET, his wife, died 2 April, 1813, aged 81.
ROBERT BARKER, their son, died 10 April, 1819, aged 43.

4　MARY ANN, wife of JOHN CLABON, died 6 April, 1829, aged 46.
MARY ANN, her daughter, died 28 October, 1823, aged 4.
JOHN CLABON above, 48 years Vestry Clerk of the parish, died 29 June, 1868, aged 77, buried in Gravesend Cemetery.

ST. ALPHEGE, LONDON WALL

Ground on the North side of London Wall

Headstones.

1.　JOHN HUXLEY, of the parish, died 24 July, 1798, aged 38.
Six of his children died young.
ELIZABETH GILES, his mother, died 21 February, 1811, aged 85.
JONATHAN HUXLEY, his son, died 2 June, 1822, aged 25.

2.　WILLIAM KING, of the parish, died 9 January, 1810, aged 43
HELEN and GEORGE KING two of his children
JAMES, his son, died 4 March, 1810, aged 10 months.
EMMA, his daughter, died 7 November, 1825, aged 19.
HANNAH ELIZABETH BOYKETT, his daughter, wife of THOMAS BOYKETT, died 12 November, 1833

ST. ANDREW'S, HOLBORN.

Ground around the Church.

Flat stones.

1. JOSEPH AP—R—, of the parish, died ————, 1830, aged 6—.

   EMILY WHITE, his daughter, died 27 ————, 1836, aged 25.

2. HENRY WATKINS, more than 40 years of the parish, died 1 September, 1800, in his 66th year.

   MARY WATKINS, his widow, died 22 October, 1801, aged 61.

3. ANTONIO PASTORELLI, died 17 July, 1848, aged 50, leaving a widow.

   JOSEPH ANTONIO PASTORELLI, his cousin, died 28 May, 1852, aged 28

4. CAROLINE, daughter of THOMAS and ————— Master WALTER ————.

5. ————, died —— December ——, aged 2 years 10 months.

   WILLIAM FRANCIS BULLOCK, died 18 January 18—, aged 1 year 6 months.

   ANN BULLOCK, died 8 March, 1833, aged 7 years 4 months.

   ANN BULLOCK, their mother, died 19 July, 1833, aged 38.

6. JOHN SCOTT, of the parish, died 4 December, 1789, aged 72.

   MARY SCOTT, his widow, died 28 July, 1804, in her 82nd year.

   ANN SCOTT, daughter of John above, died 3 March, 1809, aged 66

   PHILIPPA SCOTT, granddaughter of JOHN SCOTT, died 22 August, 1818, aged 30.

7. JOHN WENSLEY died 5 January, 1821, aged 6—.

   MARY WENSLEY, his widow, died 17 January, 1825, aged 62.

   Mrs. MARY SMITH died 2— February, 1834, aged —o years.

   Miss ANNE WENSLEY died 4 June, 1844, aged 31

8. JOHN PRYCE, died 25 ———, 180—.
   ———LY PRYCE, died 19 November, 1809.
   ———WARD PRYCE, died 15 ———, 1814.
   RACHEL PRYCE, died 23 November, 1815, aged 82.
   MARY ———LL, late wife of ———LL, of Red
   Lion Street, Holborn, and neice of ———
   PRYCE, died 2—th December 182—

9. Family vault of JAMES and ELIZABETH TROTTER, of
   Kirby Street.
   WILLIAM HENRY, their eldest son, died 26 November,
   183—, in his 31st year.
   JAMES TROTTER, above, died 6 October, 1844, in his
   67th year.
   ELIZABETH TROTTER, above, died 29 September,
   1852, aged 75.
   EDWARD, son of JAMES CHARLES TROTTER and
   grandson of above, died 1 November, 1838, aged
   20 days.
   WILLIAM CROWDER, son of WILLIAM HENRY TROTTER
   above, died 16 May, 1853, in his 21st year

ST. ANDREW UNDERSHAFT.

Ground North of the Church.

Mural Tablets.

1. WILHELM BRANDT, born 21 November, 1815, died
   6 January, 1831.
2. Mrs. ELIZABETH WALLER, died 20 January, 1798,
   aged 47.
   JOSEPH WALLER, her husband, died suddenly, 4
   September, 1815, in his 57th year.
   Mrs. SARAH SAYER, their daughter died 18 October,
   1815, in her 34th year.
   JOHN SAYER, her husband, died 10 October, 1835,
   aged 57.
   MARY ANN FYSON, wife of JOHN FYSON, of Snail-
   well, co Camb., and daughter of above JOSEPH
   and MARY WALLER, died 27 March, 1844, aged
   58

Flat stones.

3. *Crest*—a demi lion rampant couped [or] for *Strode*
   Arms—Erm., on a canton sa. a crescent arg. for
   Strode of Dorset and Somerset impaling [Arg.]
   on a bend [sa.] 3 bells [or] for *Belton*.
   SAMUEL STRODE, died 26 December, 1727, aged 52.
   Two sons and a daughter died infants.

4. Family vault of WILLIAM MORRICE of the parish

5. Vault of M DATCHELOR made at cost of MARY and
   BEATRIX and SARAH DATCHELOR for them and
   their families, 29 September, 1699.

6. *Crest*—An eagle's head couped at the neck, between
   2 wings, elevated and displayed [sa.] the whole
   resting on 2 crosses pattée for *Vansittart*.
   Arms—[Erm.] an eagle displayed [sa.] on a chief
   [gu] a ducal coronet [or] between 2 crosses
   patteé [ar.] for *Vansittart*, of Shottesbrook, co.
   Berks., impaling.
   Paly of 6 az. and arg. over all on a bend sa.,
   a sword of the 1st [hilt and pommel or] for
   Sanderson.
   PETER VAN-SITTART, eminent merchant and citizen
   of London, died ———, 1705.

7. WILLIAM WRIGHT, inhabitant of the parish, and
   one of the Fishmongers' Company, died 29 July,
   1672.
   WILLIAM, MARY, MARY, and MARTHA, his four
   children.

8. JAMES WEBSTER and brother DAVID WEBSTER,
   merchants and partners in Leadenhall Street
   JAMES, born at Dundee, 20 March, 1724, died
   28 December, 1789, at his house on Clapham
   Common.
   DAVID, born at Dundee, 31 May 1733, died in
   Leadenhall Street, 19 December 1787.
   Rev. THOMAS WEBSTER, D.D., of Bath, their
   brother.

9. Family Vault of CHARLES WINE.

10. MARY ANN MACKAY, niece of JOHN ADCOCK, of the
    parish, died 11 August, 1803.

11. CHARLES THOROLD, died 30 November, 1691.
ANNE, his wife, died 17 November, 1702

12. ELIZABETH, wife of WILLIAM MAY, of the parish,
Cooper, died 21 August, 1781, aged 57
Above WILLIAM MAY, died 13 February, 1783, aged
52.

13. Vault made for CHARLES TORRIANO and family at
cost of his widow, Mrs. REBEKAH TORRIANO,
1 October, 1723, she died 3 August, 1754,
aged 87.
Mrs. JANE DOBSON, one of the daughters of above
CHARLES and widow of JOHN JAMES DOBSON, of
the Inner Temple, died 31 March, 1793, aged 85
Miss ELIZABETH DOBSON only ————

14. THOMAS GIFFIN, of the parish, died 9 January,
1764, aged 74

15. ABRAHAM SUTTON, Merchant, lived in Flanders, in
Ghent, about 30 years and died there 24 May,
1675, in his 55th year.

16. Dr. HUMPHREY BROOKE, buried 27 November, 1693.
JOHN BROOKE, his youngest son, buried 5 April, 1687.
Mrs. ELIZABETH BROOKE, widow of above HUM-
PHREY, buried 21 March, 1711, and their
children.
HUMPHREY BROOK, M D., buried 28 October, 1718,
aged 52.
Mrs. ELIZABETH WILLIAMS, widow of ROGER WIL-
LIAMS, buried 13 February, 1748.
ROBERT BROOKE, buried 1 September, 1748, aged 76.
Mrs. SELINA SALTER, wife of THOMAS SALTER,
buried 21 January, 1754, aged 74.

17. MARGARET, wife of WILLIAM RAMSEY, died 3
December, 1788, aged 30.
Above WILLIAM RAMSEY, Secretary to the Hon
East India Company, died 30 December, 1813,
aged 64.

18. JAMES B. BOURDIEU died 4 November, 1843, aged 85
ANN, his relict, died 21 November, 1847, in her
78th year.

19 DANIEL LE SUEUR, son of DANIEL and ANN LE SUEUR,
  died 24 February, 1752, aged 5

  Above DANIEL, died 12 March, 1775.

  Above ANN, died 3 November, 1792.

20. JOHN COOKE, only son of JOHN COOKE, of Shrews-
  bury, late collector of Excise, died 6 February,
  1788, aged 42

21 DANIEL EVANS, of the parish, died 14 August, 1782,
  aged 80.

  ANNA MARIA EVANS, his wife, died 14 January, 1807,
  aged 84.

22 WILLIAM HENRY PROBEART, of the parish, died
  17 May, 1786, aged 43.

23. MARY, wife of WILLIAM PETTIT, daughter of ABEL
  MOYSEY, late of the parish, died 14 March, 1785,
  aged 67

  Above WILLIAM PETTIT, died 19 November, 1791,
  aged 70.

All the above flat stones appear to have been in the floor
of the church originally, and to have been placed in the burial
ground some thirty years ago

ST. ANNE AND ST. AGNES.

Ground around the Church.

Altar tomb.

  1. HARRIET, daughter of WILLIAM and ELIZABETH
   PRATER, of this parish, died 24 December, 1823,
   in her 17ᵗʰ year

   WILLIAM PRATER above, Director of East London
   and West Middlesex Water Companies, died
   5 February, 1838

   ———— wife of ————, died 18 November, ——
   aged 66

  Mrs. JANE LESTER, daughter of above ————

Headstones.

  2. JONATHAN HARDCASTLE, of Clerkenwell parish, died
   12 June, 1824, aged 72, leaving a widow.

WILLIAM SAMUEL JONATHAN HARDCASTLE, son of JONATHAN and MARY HARDCASTLE, died 9 April, 1793, aged 1 year 5 months.

MARY HARDCASTLE, wife to JONATHAN above, died 17 June 1828.

3. ———— of the parish, Deputy of the Ward, died 10 May, 1799, aged 78.

EDWARD ————

4. Family grave of EDWARD HENRY and MARY SANDERSON, of the Bull and Mouth. Their children —

EDWARD died 30 June, 1835, aged 10 weeks.

SAMUEL EMERY, died 18 April, 1846, aged 3½ years.

ANN HUNT, died — November, 1851, aged 11.

5. JOHN MARKS URBAIN died 30 August, 1832, aged 35.

6. Mrs. CHARLOTTE GREENWOOD, of the parish, died 8 December, 1829, in her 47th year.

FREDERICK CHARLES GREENWOOD, her son, died 16 December, 1833.

WILLIAM HENRY GREENWOOD, died 25 February, 1825, aged 11 years 7 months.

7. ANNA, wife of HUGH HUGHES, many years of the parish, died 30 April, 1839, aged 36.

8. RICHARD BREEST——, of the parish, died 15 August, 1811, in his 48th year.

ELIZABETH, his daughter, died 24 June, 1805, in her 3rd year.

9. JOHN JACKSON, of Westmoreland Buildings, died 9 August, 1836, aged 46.

JANE, wife of JOHN JUTSUM ————

10. JOHN BAILEY, died 21 May, 1836, in his 80th year.

MARY BAILEY, his wife, died ————

11. Miss MARY HARMER, died February, 1819, aged 49.

MARGARET GEORGE and WILLIAM WOODWARD all died young.

JOHN WOODWARD, died 20 September, ——

12. JULIANA, wife of THOMAS BRADSHAW ————

ST. ANNE, BLACKFRIARS.

Site of the church which was destroyed by the Great Fire of 1666, and ground near by.

Headstones.

1. WILLIAM SIMMS, of the parish, died 24 March, 1828, in his 65th year.

   FRANCIS OCTAVIUS, his son, died 7 October, 1820, aged 12

   SARAH SIMMS, his wife, died 7 January, 1834, in her 67th year

2. GEORGE MARSH, died 25 July, 1825, aged 68.

   CAROLINE ANN MARSH, his relict, died 22 December, 1830, aged 58.

   Four of their children died infants.

3. MARY, wife of PHILIP SAUNDERS DAVENPORT, died 10 November, 1813, aged 33

   MARY, wife of JOHN DAVENPORT, died 19th January, 1817, aged 50.

4. GEORGE HOW, of the parish, died 24 December, 1821, aged 28.

5. ELIZABETH, wife of JOHN TAYLOR, of the parish, died 18 September, 1827, aged —1.

6. ANN HISLOP, late of Old Change, Cheapside, died 11 August, 1823, aged 39.

   RICHARD SMEETON HISLOP, her nephew, of Wardrobe Place, Doctors' Commons, died 27 February, 1823, aged 10 months.

   MARY ANN HISLOP, died 21 May, 1830 aged 13 months.

   MARY JULIA HISLOP died 7 May, 1832, aged 39 days.

   ROBERT HISLOP, uncle to the above children, died 13 January, 1844, aged 62.

7. ————, wife of HENRY WARD, of the parish, died 20 June, 181—, aged 44.

   Eight of her children.

   HENRY WARD, above, died 11 November, 182—, aged 47.

8. MARY BEW, of the parish, died 25 October, 1820, aged 74

C

TIMOTHY BEW, her husband, died 13 March, 1794, aged 55

9. JAMES DRURY HOOK, of Shoemaker Row, in the parish, died 29 November, 1828, aged 69.

ANN, his wife, died 8 April, 1840, aged 75.

ST. BARTHOLOMEW THE GREAT.
Ground around the Church.

Mural tablets.

1. JANE, wife of ROBERT PAGE, of Chiswell Street, died 13 January, 1817, aged 57.

ROBERT, her husband, died 6 March, 1824, aged 55.

2. Mrs. JUDITH SMITH, died 16 June, 1698.

Headstones

3. JOHN JONES, many years of the parish, but late of Holloway, died 22 September, 1833, in his 62nd year.

Two of his children died infants

CATHERINE JONES, his wife, died 22 January, 1837

4. WILLIAM COOPER P——, of Yarnton, co. Oxon., died 5 June, 1816, in his 19th year.

JAMES GRAHAM, died 17 February, 1827, aged 5[1?]

5. WILLIAM JOHNSON, of the parish, died 15 October, 1814, in his 27th year.

SUSANNAH, his wife, died 28 August, 1819, in her 28th year.

ELIZABETH BENWELL, died 10 October, 1819, aged 2 weeks

Mrs. MARY HORNE HOLLAND, mother of above SUSANNAH, died 1 January, 1820, aged 56

MARY BENWELL, died 30 April, 1820, aged 7 months.

ANN HOLLAND, died 30 March, 1827, aged 28.

HARRIOT, wife of JOSEPH KNIGHT, of St George's, Hanover Square, daughter of Mrs. HOLLAND above, of the parish, died 15 January, 1829, aged 21

6. ELIZABETH, wife of THOMAS SIMPSON, late of the parish, died 20 December, 1775, in her 77th year.

   Mrs. HESTER BARRAS, her sister, died 21 December, 1775, aged 8[o?].

7. WILLIAM ELSTON, late of the parish, died 9 July, 1821, in his 70th year.

8. ALFRED, son of GEORGE and HARRIETT WEAVER, of the parish, died 20 May, 1848, aged 14 months.

9. Grave of JOHN EDWARDS, junr.

   RICHARD EDSON (?) died 7 December, 1826, aged 74

   SUSANNA, his wife, died ————

   On the footstone: R E., 1826. S.E., 1826. M.J.E., 1834

10. JOHN MILLS, of Kensington Gore, died 31 January, 1810, aged 49.

11. Mrs. ANN EDWARDS, died 21 February, 1801, aged 67. Her grandchildren :—

    ANN EDWARDS, died 14 January, 1804, aged 3 months.

    SARAH EDWARDS, died 10 December, 1810, aged 4 years 7 months

    RICHARD ADAM EDWARDS, died 13 December. 1810, aged 3.

    SARAH ANN EDWARDS, died 1 September, 1811, aged 4 months.

    GEORGE WILLIAM EDWARDS, died 12 October, 181—, aged 2 years 3 months.

    RUTH YOUNG EDWARDS, wife of JOHN EDWARDS, died 4 June, 1826, aged 42.

    JOHN EDWARDS, her husband, died 3 August, 1829, aged 60.

12. JOSEPH DANELL, of Oxford Street, Marylebone, son-in-law of late Mr BARNS, of the parish, died 24 May, 1829, aged 55.

13. JOHN SKITT, late of Warrington, co. Lanc., born 28 September, 1810, died 7 February, 1833.

14 MARY WHEELER, died 31 October, 1824, aged 74.

   DANIEL WHEELER, her husband, 68 years of the parish, died 17 July, 1834, aged 84.

C 2

MARTHA HART, their daughter, died 31 January, 1842, aged 54.

MARTHA CHARLOTTE HART, daughter of last, died 9 December, 1852, aged 40.

Two children who died infants

ANN BEWGE HOLLAND, died 15 April, 1868, aged 78, interred at Finchley, 25 April, 1868

15. ANN, wife of RICHARD RICHARDS, of the parish, died 12 August, 1793, aged 51.

RICHARD RICHARDS, above died 27 June, 1796, aged 52.

MARY, wife of ROBERT ATTENBOROUGH, late of Crown Street, Finsbury Square, and daughter of above, died 27 March, 1815, aged 33.

Two children of last who died infants

16. STEPHEN STEPHENS, died 15 August, 1804, aged 6—.

ELIZABETH STEPHENS, his wife, died 14 February, 18[15 ?].

ANN STEPHENS, mother of STEPHEN above, died ———— aged 86.

GEORGE, son of STEPHEN and ELIZABETH above, died 2 March, 1826, aged 52

17. Mrs. ELEANOR ALLEN, and 3 children who died infants

18. JOHN FLOOKS, died 11 November, 1804, aged 42.

Six of his children :—

KATHERINE MARY, died 5 November, 1789, aged 2.

JOHN, died 20 May, 1790, aged 6 months.

KATHERINE, died 9 September, 1798, aged 5 years 6 months.

JOHN, died 23 October, 1798, aged 2 years 6 months.

KATHARINE SUSANNA, died 23 October, 1804, aged 5 years 8 months.

One died in infancy.

19 SARAH, wife of SAMUEL TIBBS, of the parish, died 23 April, 1804, aged 4 [1 or 4].

SAMUEL TIBBS above, died 26 June, 1813, agee 50.

20. WILLIAM STARKEY, husband of SUSANNA STARKEY, of the parish, died 23 October, 1809, in his 44th year.

Four of their children :—

WILLIAM, died 13 July, 1789, aged 4.

HARRIOT, died 9 February, 1792, aged 4 months

EDWARD, died 7 March, 1802, aged 4 months.

HARRIOT, died 8 October, 1805, aged 6 months.

SUSANNA STARKEY, died 11 June, 1825, aged ——.

Master WILLIAM STARKEY, grandson of above, died —— September, 1823, aged 4.

Master HENRY EDWARD STARKEY, grandson of above, died ———, 183—, aged 3 [or 5].

21. MARY, wife of SAMULL MITCHELL, of the parish, died 5 May, 1806, aged 35.

SUSANNA, daughter of above, died 19th August, 1800, aged 4 months.

ANN, daughter of above, died 16 November, 1808, aged 3 years 6 months.

SAMUEL MITCHELL above, died 4 August, 1832, aged 66.

ELIZABETH STEVLNS MITCHELL, his widow, died 9 May, 1839, in her 62nd year.

22 WILLIAM TITMUSS, died 29 August, 1819, aged 54

SARAH, his wife, died 2 January, 1844, aged 75.

23. JANE, wife of L. WRATHALL, died 9 February, 1808, aged 55.

LUPTON WRATHALL, died 26 July, 1821, aged 64.

WILLIAM LUPTON WRATHALL, son of WILLIAM and ROSAMOND WRATHALL, and grandson of above, died 3 May, 1827, aged 2.

ROSAMUND WRATHALL, died ———, 1827, aged 44.

WILLIAM WRATHALL, died ———, 1841, aged 5— years.

24 JOHN ARTHORP, of High Holborn, died 27 June, 1811, aged 58.   Five of his children by his wife SARAH :—

ELIZABETH, died 1802, aged 5 years 4 months.

JOHN died, 1803, aged 11 days.

JOHN, died 1805, aged 1 year 2 months.

HANNAH, died 1808, aged 6 years 7 months.

JOHN, died 1809, aged 1 year 4 months.

Mrs. SARAH HALL, formerly Mrs. SARAH ARTHORP and wife of above, died 9 January, 1837, aged 69.

25. MARTHA, daughter of Mr. and Mrs. JOHN ARTHORP and wife of WILLIAM DAVISON, of Bread Street, solicitor, died 20 September, 1835, aged 37, a mother.

WILLIAM DAVISON above, died 28 October, 1847, aged 54.

SARAH, second wife of above, died 10 February, 1884, interred in Putney Cemetery.

26. JOSEPH BARKER, of the parish, died 3 December, 1818, aged 40

JOSEPH ALFRED BARKER died 29 June, 1824, in his 17th year.

JANE BARKER, daughter of above, died 14 May, 1825, aged 12.

27. THOMAS BATES, of the parish, died 26 May, 1819, aged 68.

MARY, his wife, died 23 February, 1843, aged 86.

28 MARTHA, wife of GEORGE SMITH, of Long Lane, Baker, died 1 December, 1819, aged 27.

GEORGE SMITH above, died 3 October, 1829, aged 52.

MARTHA SMITH, daughter, died 2 February, 1832, aged 19.

29. JOHN STEARNS died 14 April, 1808, aged 46.

30. GEORGE HASTINGS, died 23 March, 1816, aged 39.

Mrs. Sarah Compton, many years of this parish, mother-in-law of above, died 6 January, 1823, in her 81st year.

Mrs. SARAH TAYLOR, her eldest daughter, died 16 August, 1832, in her 57th year.

Mrs. ELIZABETH ————, daughter of Mrs. COMPTON above, died 1 [or 4] May, 1837, aged [58 ?].

31. SARAH, wife of GEORGE DENNESSON, of the parish, died 24 February, 1814, aged 50.

Mrs. MARY DENNESSON, Senr., died 9 May, 1798, aged 63

Mrs. SARAH DENNESSON, second wife of above, died 11 April, 1819, aged 38.

GEORGE DENNESSON above, died 28 June, 1819, aged 51.

THOMAS GALE died 2 April, 1820, in his 61st year.

32 JOHN GOODFELLOW, died 5 April, 1822, in his 39th year.

33. MARY, wife of WILLIAM BROUGH, of the parish, died 12 August, 1796, aged 48.

Two of her children CHARLOTTE and CHARLES who died infants.

WILLIAM BROUGH above, died 5 December, 1819, aged 75.

Miss Eliza BROUGH, granddaughter of above, died 5 July, 1819, aged 3.

WILLIAM PASS BROUGH, died ————

WILLIAM THOMAS BROUGH, father of last, died 13 April, 183—, aged 63.

34 JAMES MORRIS, died 13 January, 1814, aged 51.

SARAH, his wife, died 3 February, 1823, aged 71.

35 Mrs. ANN FINNEY, late of Lead Hall, co. York, died 17 May, 1802, aged 84.

Mrs. HARRIETT DUDDY, her granddaughter, died ———— 1853.

36. JOHN PARSONAGE, died 21 December 18—0, in his 55th year.

ANN, his wife, died 9 October, 1821, in her 74th year.

37 REBECCA FONTENEAU, died 7 November, 1824, aged 74

Mrs. PHŒBE MATTHEWS, daughter of Mr. JOEL BARNS, died 25 January, 1826, aged 68.

SAMUEL MATTHEWS, died 6 February, 1836, aged 5—

38. JOHN, son of WILLIAM and SARAH GILLINGWATER, of the parish, died 21 December, 1824, aged 6 months 21 days.

MARY GILLINGWATER, grandmother of above, died 16 July, 1828, aged 6—.

ISAAC GILLINGWATER, grandfather of the above John ————

39. Family grave of THOMAS and HOPE BEDFORD, of Charterhouse Lane.

ELIZABETH BEDFORD, died 18 February, 1819, aged 16 months.

ELIZABETH BEDFORD, died 9 April, 1822, aged 9 months.

40. ELIZABETH POWELL, died 1 March, 178—.
Five of her children

SARAH ANN POWELL, died ——— 180— aged 2 years 11 ———

SARAH SWANWICK, died 10 ——— 1806, aged 44

41. THOMAS JENNINGS, died 25 December, 1785, aged 68.

THOMAS, his son, died 1 January, 1786, aged 44.

JOHN, son of JOSEPH S. JENNINGS, of the parish, died 15 August, 1788, aged 7.

SARAH SOPHIA, died 6 April, 1792, aged 1 year 7 months.

SOPHIA MARGARET, died 5 February, 1794, aged 1 year 7 months

ELIZABETH, wife of above, died 31 July, 1794, aged 82.

MARY ANN, died 27 October, 1797, aged 7 weeks

WILLIAM, died 17 November, 1799, aged 4 years 8 months.

SAMUEL JENNINGS, died 2 December, 1801, aged 27.

LOUISA ANN JENNINGS, died 31 August, 1802, aged 8 months.

JOSEPH JENNINGS, died 6 August, 1807, aged 55

42. JOSEPH WAFFORNE, of the parish, died 25 February 1834, aged 59.

MARY, his wife, died 25 March, 1837, aged 62.

43 ELIZABETH, wife of JOHN THOMPSON, of No. 38, Cloth Fair, in the parish, died 22 August, 1841, in her 43rd year.

MARY, their daughter, died 31 January, 1834, aged 18 months.

44. ———, September, 177—, aged 3 years — months

ESTHER WILLIAMS, daughter of above, died 29 August, 1782, aged 31.

ANN ESTHER WILLIAMS ———.

45. ELIZABETH, wife of WILLIAM COLLINS, of Queen
   Square, in the parish, died 5 March, 1803,
   aged 45.

   WILLIAM COLLINS, above, died 20 September, 1807,
   aged 55.

Footstones.

46. To No. 40. —1799. —1787.

47 J.S. 1793. J.S. 1826. A.E. 1834. J.E. 1838.
   J.E.—. S—.

ST. BENNETT, PAUL'S WHARF.

Mural Tablet on the Church

   TIMOTHY WOOD BOLLARD, died 28 June, 1829, aged 29

   MARY WEBB, his mother, died 28 August, 1853, aged 84,
   buried in the head vault of St. Saviour's,
   Southwark.

ST. BENNETT, SHEREHOG.

Site of the Church which was destroyed by the Great Fire
of 1666.

Altar tomb.

   Family vault of MICHAEL DAVISON, died 1676.

ST. BOTOLPH, ALDERSGATE.

Ground by the Church.

Altar tombs.

1. WILLIAM BEAUMONT CRANFIELD, of Shepherd's
   Bush, co Middlesex, and landowner, of Bromley, co. Kent, died 28 July, 1836, aged 72.

   FRANCES CRANFIELD, his relict.

   GEORGE CRANFIELD, their son, died 27 November,
   1829, in his 36th year.

   JANE, their youngest daughter, died 1 May, 1840.

2. CAROLINE SUMMERS, died 24 January, 182—, in her
   —9th year.

MARY ANN, wife of FREDERICK SUMMERS, died
— August, 1829.

Stones on the ground.

3.   NATHANIEL GILBERT SCOTT, son of Rev. THOMAS
SCOTT, [formerly 'of Gawcott, Bucks., late of
Wappenham, Northants, died 11 June, 1831,
aged 16.

4   THOMAS WARD, Builder, late of St. Luke's, Cripple-
gate Without, died 23 August, 1851, aged 45
His children :—
————— WARD, died 24 July, 1834, aged 3.
————— WARD, died 11 February, 1836, aged 2.
————— WARD, died 16 April, 1838, aged 2

Headstones.

5.   MARY ANN, wife of JOHN WARD, died 30 December,
1844, aged 42.

6.   JOHN ALEXANDER TOQRE, of Bernard Street, Russell
Square, died 1— September, 1815 (or 3), aged 51.
WILLIAM HENRY TOQRE, second son of above, died
1— September, 181—, aged — months — weeks

7.   SARAH, wife of ROBERT DERRICK PINNELL, of the
parish, died 26 February, 1835, aged 30.
Their children :—
HANNAH ANN, died 3 September, 1829, aged 20
months.
GEORGE FREDERICK, died 22 September, 1832, aged
2 years 8 months.
JOHN THOMAS, died 12 October, 1832, aged 11
months 29 days.
HANNAH JANE, died 27 June, 1834, aged 14 months.
SARAH MARY, eldest daughter, died ————, aged 11.
JANE HANNAH PINNELL, died ————, aged ————
and 6 months
GEORGE ————— PINNELL, died ————, aged —
years.

8.   THOMAS AUSTIN, of the parish, died 15 April, 1831,
in his 48th year.
HANNAH, his wife, died 16 November 1811, aged 35.
Children of above Thomas :—

JOHN AUSTIN, died 3 September, 1806, aged 3 months.

THOMAS AUSTIN, died 25 June, 1807, aged 1 year and 3 weeks.

THOMAS AUSTIN, died 31 December, 1811, aged 23 months 6 days.

WILLIAM AUSTIN, died 18 April, 1819, aged 3 months 16 days.

9   Family Grave of WILLIAM and FRANCES SPRY, of Charterhouse Square.

WILLIAM SPRY, died — July, 1808, aged 6 months.

EMMA SPRY, died 8 February, 1820, aged 10 years.

FRANCES SPRY, died 7 September, 1820, aged 17 years.

JANE SPRY, died 22 February 1821, aged 19 years.

EMMA ROSE SPRY, died 18 May, 1822, aged — years 11 months — days.

—— MARY SPRY, died 10 July, 1831, aged — years.

WILLIAM HENRY SPRY, died 9 December, 1831, in his 17th year.

10   EDWARD COCKER, died ————, 1820.

11.   Mrs. SARAH PUGH, died 21 May, 1824, aged 56.

RICHARD PUGH, died 4 October, 1825, aged 58.

ANN PUGH, their daughter, died 24 October, 1825, aged 21.

MARY LEE, died 5 December, 1835, aged 47.

RICHARD CLOUDES COLE, son-in-law of RICHARD PUGH above died 16 October, 1839, aged 45.

SARAH GUSLER, friend of the above, died 3 August, 1842, aged 51.

12.   ELEANOR BLOOD, died —5 March, 181—, aged 19 months.

JOHN BLOOD, her father, died 28 ————

FRANCIS BLOOD, his son, died ————, 182—, aged 9 years — months.

13.   GEORGE JOHN DAVIES, son of HENRY and SOPHIA DAVIES, of Aldersgate Street, died 24 September, 1831, aged 4 years 2 months.

Mrs. CATHERINE ANN POTTS, his aunt, died 19 May, 1835.

14. THOMAS LOCKEY, of the parish, died ————, 1832

15. ELIZA, wife of FRANCIS HENRY GROOM, of the parish, died 1— December, 1828, aged 43.

JULIA, their daughter, died — December, 1828, aged — months

SUSANNAH LETITIA, wife of the above, born 24 February, 180—, died 14 April, 1844.

FRANCIS HENRY GROOM, died 7 February, 1848, aged 6— years

16. Miss SUSANNAH BIAGGINI, died ———— 1823, aged 17.

MAX ———— BIAGGINI, her father, died 10 November, 1830, aged 68.

Mrs. ANNE BIAGGINI, died 1—th July, 1836, aged 71.

17. THOMAS JONES, of the parish, died 23 July, 1841, aged 56

CATHERINE, his wife, died 14 October, 18—, aged 64

18. ELIZABETH, wife of WILLIAM GAISFORD, of the parish, died 10 November, 1803, aged 47.

JOHN HOGATH, late of Chiswell Street, St. Luke, died 11 March, 1787.

WILLIAM GAISFORD, died 8 July, 1808, aged 55.

19. MARY, wife of WILLIAM DODMAN, died 11 November, 1825, in her 52nd year.

Three of their children died infants.

WILLIAM DODMAN, above, died 23 November, 1830, aged 63.

20. MICHAEL COOMES, died 15 April, 1828, aged 37.

ELIZABETH, his wife, died 22 April, 1836, aged 36.

WILLIAM and THOMAS COOMES their infant children.

21. FANNY, wife of WILLIAM SNOWLEY, of the parish, died 22 November, 1837, aged 48.

22. FRANCES MARIA, youngest daughter of JOHN and SARAH LORKIN, of Aldersgate Street, died 12 November, 1852

SARAH LORKIN, above, died 26 August, 1856, aged 72.

JOHN LORKIN, Deputy, born 19 July, 1781, died 5 November, 1865, buried at the Highgate Cemetery.

23 JAMES EMERY, of the parish, died 3 May, 1832, aged 55.

24. Mrs. ANN SAVAGE, late HUMPHREYS, many years of the parish, died 3 May, 1843, aged 56.

25. Rev. EDMUND DAWSON LEIGH, died 7 March, 1845, aged 44.

EDMUND, his son, died 24 January, 1840, aged 8 years 5 months.

26. JOHN PALMER, died 21 September, 1842, in his 52nd year, a husband.

27. MARTHA, wife of GEORGE DONCAR, died — January, 1841, aged 61.

ELIZABETH, her granddaughter, aged 6.

28. SARAH, wife of THOMAS HARDING FALCON, of the parish, died — March, 183—.

29. Mrs ELEANOR LOVELAND, of the parish, died 11 December, 1773, aged 63.

WILLIAM LOVELAND, her husband, died 15 January, 1780, in his 74th year.

JOHN LOVELAND, their son, died 6 February, 1807.

30. Family grave of HENRY and HARRIOT AGATE.

———— AGATE, died ————.

———— AGATE, died ————, 1836, aged — days.

31. Family grave of PETER and MARTHA SAUBERGUE, of St. Bartholomew the Great.

PETER SAUBERGUE, died — July, 1840, aged —9 years.

MARTHA SAUBERGUE, his daughter, died April, 1842.

32. JOSHUA HOBSON, of the parish, died 5 February, 1833, aged 49.

JOSHUA HOBSON, his son, died 18 December, 1825, aged 3 months.

33. STEPHEN MINTER, late of St. Luke's parish, Middlesex, died ————, aged 42.

34. BENJAMIN, son of BENJAMIN and CATHERINE ROBIN-
    SON, of Little Britain, died ——, 1836, aged
    — months.

35. JAMES CELL, died ——, aged 5 ——.
    DINAH, his wife, died 16 December, 1820, aged 29
    MARY ANN, their child, died an infant.
    JAMES CELL, died 26 December ——, aged 66.
    ANNE CELL, died 11 February ——, aged 75.

36. RICHARD HACKWORTH, died 22 ————, 1834,
    aged 22.

37. ISAAC COLEMAN, of the parish, died 27 February,
    1833.

38. Family grave of ROBERT and CHARLOTTE BIGGAR, of
    Aldersgate Street.
    ROBERT ———— BIGGAR, their son, died 20 January,
    180[8?].
    Mrs. ANN SARAH HULKE, died 10 March, 1821.
    Mrs. CHARLOTTE BIGGAR, above, died 14 August,
    1833, aged 72.

39. WILLIAM AP—— TRENCH, son of WILLIAM TRENCH,
    died 1— November, 1810, aged — months

40. Miss CLARA BARRETT, died 16 November, 1826,
    aged 1 year 7 months
    WILLIAM BARRETT, her father, died 7 July, 1830, —.

41. FRANCIS STUCKLEY, of the parish, died 29 October,
    ——, aged 48.

42. HENRY SERJEANT, of the parish, died 31 October,
    1803, aged 60.
    ELIZABETH, his wife, died 21 November, 1815,
    aged 85.

43. JOHN MCKERRELL, late of Theobald's Road in the
    parish of St. George the Martyr, died ——, 1835.

44. EDWARD THATCHER, died 14 March, 1843, in his
    26th year.

45. JOSEPH HOOPER, of the parish, died 28 July, 1831,
    aged 4— years.
    CAROLINE, CHARLES and MA—, his children.

46. GEORGE DOWLING, of Goodman's Fields, died 10
    June, 1830, aged 80.

GEORGE, his only son, died on his passage from
Africa, died 14 October, 1824.

NICKOLSON, wife of GEORGE DOWLING, died 1 July,
1831, in her 81st year.

JANNETTE RUTHERFORD, third daughter of the above
died 10 November, 1831.

ELIZABETH GOAD, eldest daughter of above, died 8
December, 1837, aged 5—.

47 SAMUEL REDDISH, of the parish, died 10 July, 1840,
aged 45.

48. ELIZABETH, daughter of EDWARD and ANN HILL,
died 12 January, 1825, aged 30.

Footstones.

49. S.H. 1837.   E.H. 1843.   T.H. 1849.
50. E.P. 1838.   M.A.P. 1848
51. T.J. 1841.   C.J. 1844.
52. E.G. 1828.   J.G. 1822.   S.L.G. 1844.
     T.H.L. 1848.

ST. BOTOLPH, ALDGATE.
Ground around the Church.

Altar tombs.

1. MARGARET, wife of JAMES SIDNEY, died 30 May, 1801,
aged 45.

JAMES SIDNEY, above, died 12 February, 1834,
aged 74.

Ensign PHILIP SIDNEY, of the 43rd Regiment, son of
JAMES and MARGARET SIDNEY, died 11 December,
1811, aged 24, at Coimbra, in Portugal, buried
there.

Rev. JAMES SIDNEY, died 29 December, 1862,
aged 77, at Bruton, co. Somerset, buried at
Milton, Clevedon, said co.

Children who died infants :—

WILLIAM, born 8 November, 1783, died 10 September, 1785.

MARY, born 3 July, 1789, died 17 September.

MARY ANN, born 3 April, 1790, died 18 September.

MARGARET ⎫ born 12 March, ⎧ died 20 September.
ISABELLA ⎬ 1793 ⎨ died 26 September.
FRANCIS ⎭ ⎩ died 26 September.

HENRY ALGERNON, born 2 May, 1794, died 31 (*sic*) September.

Flat stones.

2. JOHN GIBBON, died 29 October, 1844, aged 79.

3. *Crest*—A dog statant.
   Arms———— a bend ————
   JOHN NEWTH, son of JOSEPH and SUSANNA NEWTH, of the parish, died 2 April, 1774.
   SUSANNA NEWTH, died — May ————

Headstones.

4. ELIZABETH, wife of WILLIAM WAND of the parish, died ———— 1800, aged —8.
   WILLIAM WAND, above, died — August, ——.
   MARY ANN WAND, died — May, ——.

5. THOMAS EBRALL, Citizen and Corn Merchant, shot by a Life Guardsman unknown, in the shop of Mr. Goodeve, Fenchurch Street, 9 April, 1810, died 17th same month, in his 24th year.
   THOMAS EBRALL, his father, died from his loss, 23 August, 1810, aged 48.

6. JOHN FAULKNER, of Queen Street, Tower Hill, died 18 July, 1846, aged 79.
   SARAH FAULKNER, his widow, died 11 May, 1850, aged 79.

7. WILLIAM ALEXANDER MACANDIE, son of JAMES and ANN MACANDIE, of the parish, died 27 September, 179[6 or 9], aged 2 years 11 weeks.
   ANN MACANDIE, above, died 27 January 1815, aged 64.

8. MARY, wife of Capt. WILLIAM LINDER, of the parish, died 25 May, 1800, aged 45.
   JOHN LINDER, son of above, died 24 December, 1802, in his 21st year.
   HENRY LINDER, son of above, died 19 October, 1811, aged 34.

Mary Linder, daughter of above, died 9 February 1817, in her 38th year.

Robert Linder, son of above, died 4 August, 1818, aged 34.

―――― Linder, daughter of above, died 2 October, 1822, aged ― months 12 days.

9   James Duff, of the parish, died 11 December 181―, aged 53.

Ann Duff, his wife, died 1 July, 1808, aged 44.

Also six of their children who died infants.

10.   Emma Mosedon, died 30 November, 1822, aged 2 years 9 months

William Henry Mosedon, her brother, died 28 November, 1824, aged 6 years 7 months.

John Wale, their uncle, died 30 August, 1835, aged 38.

11.   Hannah, daughter of John and Mary Wippell, of the parish, died 18 December, 1800, aged 18 months.

Richard, their son, died ― December, 1808, aged 7

Elizabeth Wippell, daughter of above, died ― July, 181―, aged 3.

Mary Wippell above, died ――――

12.   Martin, son of Martin and Martha Markham, of the parish, died 15 January, 1805, aged 1 year 11 months.

Henry Markham, died 29 January, 1805, aged 4 months 14 days.

Martin Markham, son of above, died ― March, ――, aged 15 months

―――― , died 5 February, ――

13.   Proud Longdill, of the parish, died 31 May, 1809, aged 60.

Mrs. Honour Wilmot, died 7 July, 1799, aged 87

14.   ―――― Wenham, daughter of ――――, of the parish, died 1 January, 1812, aged 1 year.

Caleb Wenham, father of above, died 9 May, 1814, aged 35.

15.   Charles Warden, died ― May, 1822, aged 57.

Elizabeth, his wife, died ― June, 182―, aged 5―

16. THOMAS HOBSON, citizen and blacksmith, for many years of the parish, died ———, 180—, aged 65.

17. THOMAS PARRY, of this parish, died 15 February, 1812, aged 55.
ANN PARRY, his relict, died 31 May, 1818, aged 47.
Mr EUSEBIUS LEIGH, died 23 January, 1810, aged 42.

18. Captain HUGH M———

19. CATHERINE ABIGAIL SONTAG, died 8 October, 1845, aged 21.
SARAH ELIZABETH WILLER, her sister, died 28 April, 1835, aged 7 years 6 months.

20. WILLIAM PATTERSON, died 5 April, 1824, aged 73.

21. JOHN BALMAN, Apothecary, died — December, 18—, aged 59.
Also (7 ?) of his children who died infants.

22. ROBERT CLARKSON, of the parish, died 17 September, 1813, aged —6.
ELIZABETH, his daughter, died in childhood.
HANNAH, wife of ———

23. WILLIAM BYSON, formerly of the parish, died 26 April, 1798, in his 53rd year.
JANE, his wife, died — March, 1803, in her 50th year.
WILLIAM BYSON, their son, died 30 January, ———, aged (34 ?).

24. JAMES, son of JOSEPH and ELIZABETH ———

25. GEORGE BURTON, senr., of the parish, died — January, 1796, aged 72
ANN, his wife, died 7 April, 1805, aged 76.
Mrs. MARY PEAL, sister to above GEORGE, died 16 April, 1809, aged 77.

26. JOHN KETTEL, of Minories, died 2 June, 1813, in his 44th year.

27. MARGARET, wife of ROBERT COSSEY, died 7 September, 1818, aged 36.

28. CHARLOTTE, daughter of CHARLES and MARY WHITE, of the parish, died 11 February, 1836, aged 21.
JAMES, SARAH, AMBROSE and JOHN, also children, died in infancy.

ELIZABETH WHITE, daughter of above, died 12 March, 1837, aged 28.

MARTHA AGNES WHITE, daughter of above, died 6 March, 1839, aged 26 years.

29. ANN ISABELLA ABRAHAM, daughter of ROBERT and ANN ISABELLA ABRAHAM, of the parish, died 6 November, 1800, aged 16 months

ROBERT ABRAHAM above, died 7 March, 1813, aged 47.

MARIA ABRAHAM, daughter of above, died 6 January, 1822, in her 21st year.

ANN ISABELIA ABRAHAM, above died 6 April, 1845, aged 79

30. WILLIAM JONES, died 14 January, 1819, aged 74.

31 MARY, wife of MARTIN SKELT, of the parish, died 11 May, 1844, aged 62.

MARTIN SKELT above, died 6 December, 1849, in his 71st year.

32. ———— died — March, 176—, in the —6th year of his age.

———— ELIZABETH HITCHCOCK, died 2— Ju—, 1762.

33. MARTHA, wife of THOMAS CURTIS, of Goodman's Fields, in the parish of St. Mary, Whitechapel, died 27 January, 1769, in the 30th year of her age.

34 Mrs. MARY BOYLE, died 15 January, 1816, aged 39

35. ELIZABETH, wife of JOHN FINDLEY, of the Minories, died 14 February, 1823, aged 63

JOHN FINDLEY, above, died 26 July, 1830, aged 81.

PHŒBE, wife of J. L FINDLEY, son of above, died 7 March, 1837, aged 53

JOHN LIPTROTT FINDLEY, husband of above, died 4 October, 1853, aged 7—.

36. CHARLES GLYNES, many years Vestry Clerk of the parish, died 29 December, 1803, aged 46.

CHARLES WEBSTER GLYNES, his son, succeeded his father as Vestry Clerk, and retained office until death, died 6 November, 1836, aged 51.

37. WILLIAM NICKELS GARDINER, died 7 February, 1829, in his 40th year.

38. THOMAS SMITH, of Somerset Street, Bricklayer, many years of the parish, died 10 August, 1832, aged 80.

    SARAH, his wife, died 10 March, 1829, aged 80.

    JOSEPH SMITH, their only son, died 16 November, 1816, aged 34.

39. JOHN HOPPÉ, died 11 April, 1811, aged 47.

    ELIZABETH SARAH HOPPÉ, his daughter, died 17 September, 1814, aged 21.

    LUCY, wife of HENRY CONGREVE, daughter of above, died 19 March, 1823, aged 24.

    CHARLES HOPPÉ, son of above, died 23 November, 1835, aged 30.

    MARY HOPPÉ, relict of JOHN HOPPÉ, above, died 8 June, 1845, aged 80.

40. THOMAS THORNTON, of the parish, died 18th March, 1831, aged 45.

    Mrs. ELIZABETH THORNTON ———

41. SAMUEL LAMBERT, died 3 March, 1781, aged 50.

    Mrs SARAH ———.

42. ROBERT BENDALL, of the parish, died 7 March, 1792.

    LUCY BENDALL, his wife, died 27 March, 1800, aged —9.

Foot stone.

43. G.L. 1792.   E.L. 1804.   J.W. 1814.

ST. BOTOLPH, BISHOPSGATE.

Ground around the Church.

Altar tomb.

Crest—An arm embowed in armour [ppr.] holding in the gauntlet a falchion [arg] hilt [or] for *Rawlins*

Arms—[Sa] 3 swords barwise, points to the sinister [arg.] hilts and pommels [or] for *Rawlins*

1. Sir WILLIAM RAWLINS, Knt., born 24 July, 1752, died 26 March, 1838.   Seventy years of the

parish. Fifty years a Common Councilman and many years Deputy of the Ward. Treasurer of the City of London Workhouse and of the Ward Schools. Sheriff of London and Middlesex, 1801-2. Gave £1,000 for support of said Schools year previous to his decease.

MARY RAWLINS, relict of Lieut. WILLIAM RAWLINS, of 13th Regt. of Light Infantry, died 23 March, 1836, aged 35

Flat stones.

2. GEORGE HEATH, of the parish, died 31 May, 1821, aged 56.

MARY HEATH, his wife, died 20 October, 1843, aged 82.

WILLIAM, their son, died 6 June, 1843, aged 46.

GEORGE, their eldest son, died 1st October, 1858, aged 68, buried at Highgate.

MARGARET HEATH, wife of GEORGE HEATH, died 15 January 1882, aged 94, buried at Highgate.

MARY ANN SMART, only daughter of GEORGE and MARY HEATH, above, died 12 October, 1878, aged 84, buried at Highgate.

Children of GEORGE and MARGARET HEATH :—

GEORGE WILLIAM, born October, 1825, died 8 March, 1878, buried at Highgate

ELIZABETH MARY, born April, 1827, died 24 June, 1894, buried at Highgate.

THOMAS, born October, 1830.

MARGARET, born July, 1832.

WILLIAM HENRY, born November, 1833, died 5 March, 1880, buried at Coulsdon.

JAMES, born August, 1838, died 13 January, 1883, at Christchurch, New Zealand.

3. ARTHUR CLARKE, of the parish, died 22 August, 1834, in his 44th year.

WILLIAM WISEMAN CLARKE, buried in Eltham churchyard, co. Kent, in his 22nd year.

THOMAS JUDKINS CLARKE, buried at Kensal Green, 1850, in his 37th year.

ARTHUR JAMES CLARKE, buried at Kensal Green, 1855, in his 31st year.

4. CHARLES WEBB, of the parish, died 25 June, 1832, aged 56.

ELIZABETH WEBB, his wife, died 10 January, 1838, aged 62, had issue.

5. NATHANIEL ROGERS, died 10 February, 1810, aged 69.

SUSANNA, his wife, and their children SUSANNA and MARTHA

Stone placed by his grand-nephew, NATHANIEL ROGERS, M.D , 1868

ST. BRIDE, or BRIDGET.

Ground around the Church

Flat stones.

1. Mrs. JANE WARNER, wife of ——ARD WARNER, died 3 April, 1798, aged 34.

MARY WARNER, wife of above, died 29 January, 1803, aged 27

Mr S. S. WARNER, above, died 27 May, 1829, aged 65

2 HARRIOT KENCH, daughter of JOHN and DEBORAH KENCH, of the parish, died 6 December, 1807, in her 23th year.

MATILDA KENCH, died an infant.

3. WILLIAM BROOKES, born 30 November, 1789 ; died 2 November, 1869 ; buried at Harlington, Middlesex.

ELIZABETH LOUISA AUGUSTA, his wife, born 6 March, 1787 ; died 15 March, 1852 ; buried here.

Their children .—

WILLIAM, born 12 January, 1812 , died 12 December, 1812 , buried here

JOSEPH, born 22 January, 1824 ; died 23 June, 1824; buried at Tetbury, co. Gloucestershire.

ANN, born 17 January, 1822 , died 18 October, 1824 ; buried here.

WILLIAM, born 16 December, 1818 ; died 1 December, 1838 ; buried here

SARAH, born 31 May, 1828 ; died 3 June, 1849 ; buried here

Headstones laid down.

4 SARAH, wife of W. DAVIS, of the parish, died 27 November, 18—6.

WILLIAM DAVIS, above, died 26 January, 1838, in his 69ᵗʰ year.

ANN DAVIS, ————

5 WILLIAM PITT, son of THOMAS and ANN JOLLEY, of the parish, died — March, 1828

Mrs ANN JOLLEY, died ——————, 184—

6 GEORGE, son of GEORGE and JANE ELIZABETH BAKER, of Ludgate Hill, died 12 February, 1817, aged 16 months

JANE, daughter of above, died 10 August, ——, aged 9 months.

THOMAS, son of above, died 25 February, ——, aged 12 months

ANN, daughter of above, died 11 February, 18—, aged — months 13 days

MARGARET, daughter of above, died 10 January, ——, aged 2 years 6 weeks

JANE, daughter of above, died — June, 18—

THOMAS BAKER, son of above, died — April, 18—.

SUSANNA GRAHAM, daughter of above, died — December, ——

7. CHARLOTTE, wife of RICHARD THOMPSON, of the parish, died 13 April, 182—, aged 26 **years**

SARAH ELIZABETH CHARLOTTE THOMPSON, died 10 November, 1832, aged 3 years 10 months.

RICHARD HENRY THOMPSON, died 10 December, 1832, aged 1 year 10 months

Children of RICHARD THOMPSON, above, and SARAH MARY his wife.

CHARLES GEORGE, son of above, died 1 June, 1841, aged 18 months

SARAH MARY THOMPSON, wife of RICHARD THOMPSON,
above, died 1 September, 1841, aged 39.

RICHARD THOMPSON, above, died 24 November,
1846, aged 54

ST. CATHERINE CREE.
Ground North of the Church.

Altar tomb.

1. *Arms*—(Arg) a saltier engrailed (sa) for *Middleton*
   impaling (Arg) on a fess between 3 saltires (az.)
   an (anchor) between 3 (lions' heads erased or)
   for *Gale.*

   JOHN MIDDLETON, of the parish, died — March ——,
   aged 4—.

   Four of his children :—

   MARY MIDDLETON, died 2— December, 17—.

   LYDIA MIDDLETON, died 1— July, 17—2.

   LYDIA MIDDLETON, died 15 January, ——.
   And another.

   LOYD MIDDLETON, died 1— May, 17—, aged 36.

   JASPER GALE MIDDLETON, died 1— October, 177—,
   aged —6.

   ELIZABETH MIDDLETON, died 2— February, 1792,
   aged 7—.

   GALE MIDDLETON left 500 £3 per cent. to Aldgate
   Ward School on condition of keeping this tomb
   in repair

Headstones.

2. ELIZABETH, wife of JOHN TURNER of the parish, died
   4 August, 1850.

3. GEORGE FOSTER, died ————, 1837, aged 45

   ALFRED AUGUSTUS FOSTER, his son, died ————,
   182—, aged 6.

   HENRY FOSTER, his youngest son, died 11 October,
   182—, aged 4 months.

   MARTHA FOSTER, his wife, died 22 ————, 18—

   GEORGE FOSTER, his son, died — June, ——, aged 32.

CHRIST CHURCH, NEWGATE.
Ground around and near the Church.

Mural tablets.

1. JOHN MALLCOTT, Citizen and Mercer, of this parish, died 21 January, 1766, in his — year.

Altar tombs

2. Family Vault of CALEB WELCH COLLINS, 1832 ——.
3. HENRY SCRIMSHAW, died 30 March, 1765, aged 42.

  MARY CORK, many years of this parish, wife of above, also late wife of EDMUMD CORK, of the parish, died 13 April, 1784, aged 62.

  WILLIAM SCRIMSHAW, died 8 November, 1785, in his 29th year

  HENRY SCRIMSHAW, died 24 November, 1808, aged 47.

  TABITHA, wife of EDMUND CORK, died 10 January, 1810, aged 67.

  MARY, wife of EDMUND CORK, died 9 April, 1815, aged 48

4. MARY ANN, relict of JOHN LUFFMAN, died 21 August, 1842, aged 67.

  ELIZA JANE, wife of ALFRED LUFFMAN, of St Bride's, buried in Wetherden Churchyard, co. Suffolk, born 13 November, 1814, died 13 April, 1842.

Flat stones.

5. ELIZABETH MALLCOTT, died 26 June, 1817, aged 67.

  LOUISA SUSANNA MALLCOTT, died 25 December, 1826, aged 41

  J. M., 1849

  JOHN MALLCOTT, many years of this parish, died 22 December, 1850, aged 73.

6. I.M., 1766.   A.M., 177—.   E M., 1777.

  I.M., 1779.   C.M., 1779.   A.M., 179—.

  I.M , 1807   L M , 1807   G M., 181 (0 or 6).

7. Family grave of JOHN and CATHERINE LOGAN of the parish

  JOHN, son of the above, died 15 May, 1813, aged 2.

  ALEXANDER DICKSON, brother of Catherine above died 29 September, 1814, aged 28

ALEXANDER LOGAN, son of above, died 27 May, 1818, aged 1 year 4 months.

JOHN LOGAN above died 12 April, 1831, aged 52.

CATHERINE LOGAN above, died 9 February, 1873, aged 89, buried at Bow Cemetery.

ROBERT LOGAN, son of above, died 17 February, 1873, aged 54, buried at Bow Cemetery.

8. ARTHUR B———, and Sarah his wife, and six children and eight grandchildren.

MARY S———, grandmother of above ARTHUR and Sarah B———, buried 17 March, 1791.

9. GEORGE, son of WILLIAM and ANN WOOD.

JOHN WOOD, their son, died 16 February, 184—, aged 30

10. WALTER MATTHEWS, of Newgate Street, died 29 October, 1796, aged 66.

ANN, his widow, died 9 December, 180(3 or 5), aged 68.

WALTER, their son, died 7 May, 1768, aged 4 months

11. REBECCA, wife of JAMES PLUMMER, of Newgate Street, died 2 February, 1816, aged 44.

ESTHER, their daughter, died 4 April, 1813, aged 3.

JAMES PLUMMER above, died 13 July, 1823, aged 58.

WILLIAM PLUMMER, his son, died 18 June, 1828, aged 19.

JOHN PLUMMER, another son, died 15th October, 1832, aged 29.

12. MICHEAL NORTH.

13. RANCEFORD TOOKEY, Commander, R N., died 13 January, 1837, aged 79

RANCEFORD and JOHN CALCRAFT TOOKEY, sons of above.

14. PHILIP TRIGG, of Newgate Street, in the parish, died 31 December, 1798, aged 64.

ELIZABETH, his wife, died 15 February, 1803, aged 73.

MATTHEW TRIGG, of Islington, their son, died 11 December, 1847, aged 85.

Headstones.

15. ANNE MARIA, wife of JAMES WILKINSON, of Newgate Street, died 9 August, 1827, aged 32.

16. JANE CLARKE COBB, daughter of THOMAS and SUSANNA COBB, died 10 February, 1795, aged 1 year 9 months.

Mrs CATHERINE CLARKE, grandmother to above, died 26 March, 1818, aged 80.

17. SAMUEL WILLIAMS, died 24 January, 1810, aged 55.

Miss BETTY WILLIAMS, died 14 March, 1842, aged 62.

Mrs. CHARLOTTE WILLIAMS, died 12 September, 1844, aged 78.

Miss MARY WILLIAMS, died 12 January, 1852, aged 82.

18. CAPEL SCUDAMORE, youngest son of CAPEL and ANN SCUDAMORE, of the parish, died 23 September 18[34 ?] aged 15.

19. RICHARD OLIVER, died 1 January, 1809, aged 64.

ANN OLIVER, his relict, died 1 February, 1802, aged 65.

JOHN REEVE, died 20 October, 1810, aged 43.

THOMAS and SARAH, children of ————

ANN, relict of JOHN REEVE, died — December, 1817, aged 82.

ELIZABETH, wife of HENRY ———— and daughter of above, died 1— April, 1818, aged —.

20. JANE, daughter of THOMAS COLE of the parish, died 21 October, 1846, in her 8th year.

————, wife of THOMAS COLE above, died ————, 1850, ————.

GROUND IN KING EDWARD STREET.

Headstones.

1. EDWARD SABINE, of the White Horse, Warwick Lane, died 19 May, 1831, aged 43

2. GEORGE, son of GEORGE and FRANCES JOULES, died 2 December, 18—, aged 2 years 23 days.

3 MATILDA CAROLINE, daughter of WILLIAM and MARY
  HONEY of the parish, died 21 February, 1831,
  aged 3 years 11 months.

  CHARLES HONEY, died 20 November, 1832, aged
  1 year 11 months.

  MARY ANN HONEY, died 1 August, 1833, aged 5
  months.

  JOHN WASSELL HONEY, died 27 August, 1835, aged 7.

4. ELIZABETH, wife of RALPH CARR SPOONER, died 12
  March, 1831, aged 39

5. Miss ELIZA WINTER, died 22 July, 1838, in her
  20th year.

  Mrs ANN HUMPHREYS, her aunt, died 11 December,
  1832, aged 54

  MARY ANN HONEY, died — December 1838, aged 21,
  friend of E W. above and daughter of the late
  Mr. H. HONEY, of Christ Church parish.

6 JOHN SMITH, late of the island of Grenada, died
  10 October, 1833, in his 35th year.

  STEPHEN ALFRED PALMER, died 31 March, 1838,
  aged 32

7. RICHARD GADD, died 25 February, 1824, aged 53.

  RICHARD GADD, his son, died—October, 1824, aged 25.

  MARGARET GADD, wife of above, died 25 May, 1849,
  in her 75th year.

8 ALEXANDER CALEY, died 22 March, 1831, aged 41

  HUGH PRICE, died 15 July, 1828, aged 55

  MARGARET JANE PRICE, daughter of last, died
  3 August, 1832, in her 25th year

  JANE MARGARET CALEY, died 3 September, 1835,
  aged 10.

  Mrs. MARY PRICE, died 17 August, 1839, aged 76.

  Family grave of WILLIAM JOHN and THOMAS BISHOP.

  WILLIAM JOHN BISHOP, died 14 May, 1838, in his
  35th year.

10 Mrs RACHEL PASCO, died 9 January 1819, in her
  96th year

  SARAH HONEY, died 25 May, 1825, aged 13.

  ROBERT HONEY, died — May, 1829, aged 17.

  HENRY HONEY, their father, died ————.

ST. CLEMENT, EASTCHEAP
Ground around the Church

Altar tombs.

   1. JOHN POYNDER, of the parish, died 11 April, 1800, aged 48.

    All four of his children who died in infancy.

   2. SAMUEL MOXON, died ———, 1822, aged 72.

Headstones

   3. ROBERT WILLIAM MORRICE, son of ROBERT EDMUND and JANE MORRICE, of the parish, died 8 December, 1846, aged 2 years 4 months 4 days.

   4. WILLIAM STRONG, of the parish, died 7 August, 1839, aged 40.

ST. DUNSTAN'S IN THE EAST
Ground around the Church

Mural Tablet.

   1. Four children of JOHN and CHARLOTTE ANN VON DER HEYDE.

    CATHERINE ELIZABETH, died 7 May, 1830, aged 4 years 4 months.

    CHRISTOPHER, died 8 May, 1830, aged 2 years 9 months.

    LOUISANA, died 15 May, 1830, aged 11 months 2 days.

    GEORGIANA, died 16 May, 1830, aged 6 years.

Altar tombs.

   2. MARY Co———AY, died — February, ——, aged 39.

    WILLIAM VAUGHAN, of London, Merchant, born in the parish, 22 September, 1752, died in Fenchurch Street, 5 May, 1850.

    SAMUEL and SARAH VAUGHAN (formerly SARAH HALLOWELL) his parents buried in South aisle of church.

    SARAH and BARBARA EDDY VAUGHAN his sisters.

   3. JOHN HUNTER's Faculty vault, July, 1820.

    JOHN HUNTER, died 15 January, 183(3 or 8), aged 70.

Flat stones.

4. THOMAS HALE, died 12 May, 1845, aged 58, upwards of 38 years an inhabitant of the parish.

5. BENJAMIN BALDRY FARROW, of the parish, died 22 December, 1841, aged 69.

Headstones.

6. ELIZABETH MARSH, died 11 January, 1822, aged 40

7. GEORGE COOPER, Deputy of Bridge Ward, died 26 July, 1798, aged 83.
ANN, his wife, died 22 May, 1822, aged 70.
ALICE, wife of THOMAS COOPER, of Summit Lodge, Upper Clapton, died 6 January, 1835, aged 48

8. SUSANNAH, wife of SAMUEL JONES, of Peckham, co. Surrey, died — March, 1819, aged 69.
———— of JAMES BAYLISS and of her children CELIA MARIA and JAMES JONES.
Mr. ———— SAUNDERS.

9. THOMAS RUSTON, of the parish, died 1— January, 180—, aged —3 years.

10. THOMAS ANSTED, many years resident in the parish, died 30 October, 1846, in his 83rd year.

11. Mrs. MARY DARBY, died 1 March ————, aged 39.

12. Children of JOHN and MARY ANN GILMAN :—
FRANCIS ELLIS, died 7 May, 1807, aged 7 months
MARY ANN, died 15 June, 1808, aged 6 months
FRANCIS ALLEN, died 10 August, 1814, aged 10 months.
Above Mrs MARY ANN GILMAN, died 22 February, 1825, aged 48

13. THOMAS SANDERS, of Water Lane, son of THOMAS and ELIZABETH SANDERS, of the parish, died 15 July, 1835, in his 50th year.

14. NATHANIEL TAYNTON, died 8 August, 1800, aged 29.
ANN TAYNTON, his dau', died 30 September, 1800, aged 6 months.
HUGH TAYNTON, his son, died 15 May, 1817, aged 20 years 6 months
SARAH TAYNTON, wife of above NATHANIEL, died 2 April, 1833, in her 61st year.

15. THOMAS SANDERS, of the parish, died 26 April, 1791, aged 51.

ELIZABETH SANDERS, his wife, died at Reigate, co. Surrey, 16 June, 1798, aged 58.

16. ALEXANDER FORBES, of H M. Customs, died 4 October, 1835, in his 75ᵗʰ year.

ELIZABETH SUNLEY, his daughter, died 10 May, 1839, aged 31

——— FORBES, his son, died 10 December, 1839, aged 36.

GEORGE SUNLEY, husband of above ELIZABETH, died 23 November, 1842, aged 38.

ELIZABETH FORBES ———.

17 MARIA, wife of JAMES NAYLOR, of Strood, co. Kent, died 9 June, 1839, aged 37.

GEORGE, her son, died 4 February, 1841, aged 2 years 10 months

Above JAMES NAYLOR, died 5 October, 1846, aged 76.

18. NATHAN PARKER, late of St. John's, ———.

19. WILLIAM COLEMAN, 72 Lower Thames Street, died 31 March, 183(1 or 4).

ST DUNSTAN'S IN THE WEST.
Ground in Bream's Buildings.

Headstones.

1. SAMUEL MARSHALL, second son of EDWARD and ANNE MARSHALL, died 27 May, 1631, aged 2.

ANNE MARSHALL, eldest daughter, died 21 June, 1635, aged 1 year 9 months

NICHOLAS MARSHALL, third son, died 5 December, 1635, aged 5 years 6 months

2 JOSEPH ———, of the parish, died December

———

WILLIAM WILSON, son of above, died 12 May, 1725.

Mrs. ELIZABETH WILSON, daughter of above, died 17 October, 1730.

Mrs. ANN WILSON.

3. Repaired 1820 under the will of Mrs. ANN WILSON, remainder broken away.

4. ELIZABETH ANN MUDGE JAMES, wife of WILLIAM JAMES, late of Gough Square, in the parish, died 22 May, 1812, in her 27th year

5. Mrs. ANN BROWN, died 15 February, 1827, aged 63.

   WILLIAM ROSSE, died — May, 1794, aged 5—.

   WILLIAM RYTON, ———— ————, aged 67.

6. *Arms*—a chev. between 3 crowns, 2 and 1 for ————.

   WILLIAM RACKETT, died 12 October, 1836.

   HENRY HOLMES, grandson of above, died 11 January, 1837, aged 1 year 8 months.

7. THOMAS MARSH [?] and SUSAN or SARAH, wife.

8. Mrs. ELIZABETH HILLS, died 23 January, 1838, aged 73?

   JAMES HILLS, her husband, died 28 January, 1838, aged 62.

   HENRY HILLS, their son, died 22 February, 1838, aged 30.

9. EDWARD CANE, of the parish, died 8 November, 183(8?), aged 50.

   EDWARD CANE, his son, died 20 July, 1838, aged 25.

Footstones.

10. —C., 1841. T.C., 1837. H.C., 1845.

11. S.M., 1831. T.M., 1832 (probably of No. 7).

ST. EDMUND THE KING AND MARTYR.

Ground in rear of the Church.

Mural tablet.

1. JAMES GOODSON, of St Mary, Woolnoth parish, died 15 January, 1797, aged 48.

   CATHERINE GOODSON, his wife, died 18 March, 1841, aged 84

   JAMES, their son, died 23 July, 1782, aged 1 year 10 months.

   GEORGE, their son, died 17 May, 1789, aged 3.

CAROLINE, their daughter, died 20 July, 1842, aged 48.

CHARLOTTE, their daughter, died 27 January, 1847.

CATHERINE GOODSON, their eldest daughter, died 17 March, 1851, aged 67, buried in Nunhead Cemetery. Her surviving sister Harriett referred to.

Headstone.

2. MARY SCHOLEY, died 20 July, 1738, aged 42.

ST. ETHELBURGA.

Ground in rear of the Church.

Mural Tablets.

1 MARY ANN PEARSON, daughter of THOMAS and MARY PEARSON, of the parish, died 11 November, 1810, aged 25.

EDWARD, their son, died 28 March, 1817, aged 25.

JANE PEARSON, their 2nd daughter, died 5 July, 1817, aged 2—.

Mrs MARY PEARSON above, died 27 October, 182—, aged 63.

THOMAS PEARSON above, died 2 November, 1827, aged 74.

2. ELIZABETH, wife of JOHN SHEPHERD, of the parish, died 6 April, 1811.

FREDERICK, and ELIZA SHEPHERD, 2nd daughter of above, died infants.

JOHN SHEPHERD above, died 20 June, 1817

LOUISA FRANCES and ROBERT, grandchildren of above, died infants.

Mrs SARAH COLLEY, daughter of above, died — September, 1832, aged 36

LOUISA MARGARET SHEPHERD, died — April, 1834, aged 9 years 2 weeks

3 ANN, wife of JAMES NICHOLSON, of the parish, died 2 July, 1817, aged 26

4. MARGARET GORDON, died 4 December, 1827, aged 49.

E

5. STEWART KYD, of Stepney Green, died 11 October, 1833, in his 33rd year.

STEWART KYD, his son, died 22 November, 1834, in his 6th year.

WILLIAM TAYLOR, of Mile End, his uncle, died 4 October, 1836, in his 67th year.

FRANCES KYD, his mother, died 4 October, 1838, in her 77th year.

ANN CATHERINE, wife of STEWART KYD above, died 3 December, 1872, aged 70, buried in Hammersmith Cemetery.

ST. GEORGE, BOTOLPH LANE.

Ground South of the Church since demolished.

Mural tablets.

1. JONAS BATEMAN, of the parish, Orange Merchant, died 21 March, 1807, aged 44.

MARTHA BATEMAN, his widow, died 15 December, 1841, aged 87.

2. Mrs. SUSANNA EVERITT, late of Charles Street, Horsleydown, died 15 January, 1826, aged 30.

Mrs. SUSANNA ROME, her mother, died 14 February, 1827, aged 58

SARAH ELIZABETH ROME, daughter of last, died 4 May, 1828, aged 30.

JOSEPH ROME, father of last, died 12 July, 1836, in his 73rd year.

3. JOHN BEARDSLEY, of the parish, died 17 April, 1732, aged 34.

4. HECTOR BARNES, died 12 May, 1812, aged 54.

ANNE INNOCENT BARNES, his wife, died 30 May, 1828, aged 72.

Three grandchildren of above :—

ANNE MARIA HOWTON and MARY ANNE BARNES died infants.

EMILY CASSANDRA BARNES, died 22 March, 1826, aged 3.

Mrs. MARY BARNES, mother of above children, died 12 January, 1832, aged 43

5. WILLIAM DODDS, of the parish, died 21 October, 1789, aged 73.

Mrs CICELY STOKES, his daughter, died 27 August, 1822, aged 72.

6. Mrs. ANN PICKARD, died 10 May, 1803, aged 45.

Mrs. SARAH WHITEHOUSE, niece to Mr. WILLIAM PICKARD, died 19 January, 1807, aged 34.

ELIZABETH WHITEHOUSE, daughter of above, died 25 July, 1800, aged 14 months 10 days.

WILLIAM PICKARD, husband to ANN PICKARD above, died 23 June, 1810, aged 59.

ELIZABETH CAMPION WHITEHOUSE, died 17 May, 1812, aged 1 year 11 months 15 days.

Mrs. ANN WHITEHOUSE, died 17 June, 1817, aged 38.

7. WILLIAM, son of JOHN and FANNY WRIGHTSON of the parish, died 31 December, 1821, aged 1 year 10 months.

WILLIAM, son of above, died 25 April, 1827, aged 2 years 2 months.

LEONARD WRIGHTSON, of Upper Thames Street Ironmonger, cousin of above, died 25 September, 1828, aged 43.

MARY WARDE WRIGHTSON, died 17 July, 1832, aged 1 year.

MARY ANN WRIGHTSON, died 24 May, 1838, aged 7 months.

FANNY WRIGHTSON, mother of above, died 5 July, 1839, aged 45.

ST. GILES, CRIPPLEGATE.
Ground around the Church

Altar Tombs.

1. Mrs. ALICE STAINES, died 6 December, 1779 in her 67th year, erected by WILLIAM STAINES, her son, mason, of the parish.

SARAH, EDWARD, SARAH, WILLIAM, ALICE, MARY,
THOMAS and MARY, children of WILLIAM and
MARY STAINES, who died infants

WILLIAM STAINES, junr., died 13 August, 1784, aged
22 years 3 months.

Mrs. MARY STAINES, mother of above, died 1 July,
1792, in her 66th year.

ELIZABETH, daughter of WILLIAM and HENNE
MARIA STAINES, died 18 October, 1796, aged
8 months 3 weeks.

Lady HENNE MARIA STAINES died 6 August, 1803,
in her 35th year.

Sir WILLIAM STAINES, Knt , many years Alderman of
Cripplegate Ward, and Lord Mayor of London
1801, died 11 September, 1807, in his 77th year.

JOHN STAINES, son of Sir WILLIAM and Lady HENNE
MARIA STAINES, died 16 April, 1823, in his
26th year, leaving an only sister.

2. URIAH BRYANT, many years of this parish, died 10
December, 1840, in his 60th year.

ANN, his wife, died — August, 1841.

ANN, daughter of ADAM U. BRYANT and grand-
daughter of above, died 2— January, 18—,
aged — months — days.

ABBY BRYANT, wife of ————.

Mural tablets

3, JOHN, son of JOHN and MARY PATRICK, formerly of
the parish, but late of Islington.

MARY PATRICK, above, died 27 February, 1797,
aged 57.

SARAH, wife of THOMAS JONES, elder daughter of
above JOHN and MARY PATRICK, died 3 October,
1805, aged 36.

JOHN PATRICK, last named, died 17 October, 1816,
aged 74.

CHARLES, youngest son of GEORGE NOTLEY and
MARY his wife, and grandson of last named
JOHN PATRICK, died 18 August, 1839, aged 32.

GEORGE NOTLEY, above, died 3 September, 1841,
aged 86.

MARY, relict of GEORGE NOTLEY above, younger daughter of JOHN and MARY PATRICK, died 26 June, 1858, aged 85, buried in Highgate Cemetery

4. Rev. WILLIAM HOLMES, Vicar of the parish.

WILLIAM EMES, late of Bowbridge Field, co. Derby, died 13 March, 1803, aged 74.

WILLIAM, son of WILLIAM and SARAH HOLMES, died 13 May, 1803, aged 8 days

SARAH, daughter of same, died 22 March, 1805, aged 4 months.

JOHN, son of JOHN and REBECCA EMES, died 16 January, 1806, aged 6 months.

JOHN, second son of same, died 23 ————, 1806, aged 5 months.

JOHN EMES, died 12 May, 18—, aged 45 years.

Flat stones.

5. JONE, wife of Dr. JOHN WILSON, died 16 July, 1624, had issue by him five sons and four daughters. Erected by her daughter R B. 1674.

6. MARTHA SARAH HALSE, died 8 July, 1826, aged 63.

EDWARD HALSE, her husband, of The Crescent, Jewin Street, died — December, 1850, aged 80.

7. JOHN STEVENS, many years of the parish, died 8 January, 1818, in his 73rd year.

ANN STEVENS, his widow, died 22 April, 1818, aged 79.

JOSEPH PULLEN, their son-in-law, died 17 May, 1837, in his 66th year.

ANN PULLEN, his relict, daughter of above, died 24 May, 1847, in her 66th year

8. Family grave of J. and H. NIND, of the parish.

9. FRANCIS STRONG, 59 years of the parish, died 12 March, 1784.

ELIZABETH, wife of THOMAS STRONG of the parish, died 28 May, 1787, aged 50

THOMAS STRONG, F.A., Vestry Clerk of the parish 20 years, died 19 November, 1794, in his 59th year.

FRANCIS STRONG, of the Custom House, second son
of above FRANCIS, died 10 January, 1798, in his
61ˢᵗ year.

10. ——————————————, died 15 March, —— in his
73ʳᵈ year.

MARGARET ROBINSON, his daughter, widow of WIL-
LIAM ROBINSON, died 10 April, 1832, in her
66ᵗʰ year.

JOSEPH POULTNEY, son of above JAMES and PAVEY
POULTNEY, died 28 February, 1835, aged 76.

11. WILIIAM ROBSON, of the parish, died 16 March,
1823, in his 64ᵗʰ year

FREDERICK THOROWGOOD, son-in-law of above, died
28 May, 1834, aged 47.

MARY, his widow, died 9 February, 1835, aged 48

Mrs MARY ANN SOPHIA HUNT, eldest daughter of
F. and M. THOROWGOOD, died 29 July, 1842, in
her 31ˢᵗ year

Mrs ANN ROBSON, widow of above WILLIAM
ROBSON, died 25 August ——.

12. DAINGERFIELD TAYIOR, many years of the parish,
and Treasurer of the Boys' Charity School of
same, died 6 June, 1788, in his 74ᵗʰ year.

13. Mrs. JULIAN WILLATS, wife of THOMAS WILLATS,
died 25 February, 1826, aged 67.

THOMAS WILLATS, above, died 27 June, 1831, in his
78ᵗʰ year.

THOMAS WILLATS, his son, died 30 June, 1831,
aged 38.

14. ROBERT E. STEELE, of 21, Moor Lane, in the
parish, died 3 January, 1836, aged 39.

EDWIN STEELE, his son, died 11 August, 1839,
aged 19

MARY ANN, wife of above R. E STEELE, died
17 April, 1844, in her 63ʳᵈ year

15. JOSEPH JACKSON, many years of this parish, died
7 May, 1799, aged 77.

16. ——————, wife of WILLIAM FREEMAN, of the parish,
died ——————, 1785, aged 29

William Freeman, above, died 12 November, 1795, aged 50

17. Josias William Whitcombe, died 3 October, 1839, aged 70.

8. John Atkinson, died 18 January, 1843.

19. ——s Dawson Lea, died 4 July, 1822.

—— Dawson Lea, —— 1824, died 13 June, 1825.

20. Anne, wife of William Nicolls, died 1 August, 1753, aged 50.

William Nicolls above, of Magdalen College, Cambridge, died ——————

21. Elizabeth, wife of David Bucklet of the parish, born 20 January, 1771, died 4 May, 1790

22. John Johnson, of the parish, died 27 April, 1833, in his 68th year.

Phillis Johnson, his wife, died 11 November, 1839.

23. Edward Kirby died 5 July, 1817, aged 46.

24. ——————— ———— ——————.

Thomas Peter Earnshaw, son of Peter Earnshaw, of the parish, and Ann, his wife, and grandson of above, born 6 May, 1792, died 2 January, 1799

25 Susannah, wife of James Hopwood, of Christ Church, Surrey, died — January, ——, in her 70th year.

26 Mary, wife of ———as Smith Brewer, many years of Whitecross Street, in the parish, died

27 Benjamin Geary, of the parish, died ——————

28. ——————— wife of ———m Stebbing, of Whitechapel, late of the parish, died 21 March, 1822, in her 54th year.

Elizabeth, her daughter, died 22 April 182—, aged 23

29 William Pinder, of the parish, died 11 October, 1784

30 Elizabeth, wife of Robert Meacock, of the parish, died 2 January, 1821.

31. Thomas Wright, of the parish, died — September, ——, aged 58.

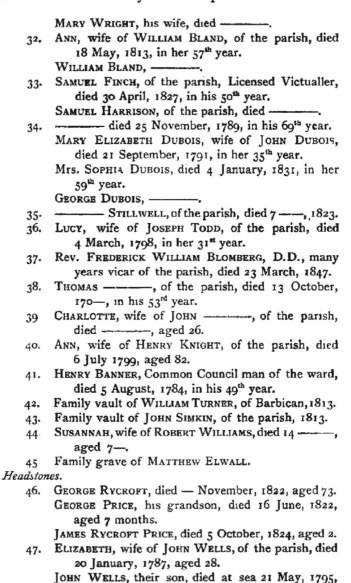

MARY WRIGHT, his wife, died ————.

32. ANN, wife of WILLIAM BLAND, of the parish, died 18 May, 1813, in her 57th year.

WILLIAM BLAND, ————.

33. SAMUEL FINCH, of the parish, Licensed Victualler, died 30 April, 1827, in his 50th year.

SAMUEL HARRISON, of the parish, died ————.

34. ———— died 25 November, 1789, in his 69th year.

MARY ELIZABETH DUBOIS, wife of JOHN DUBOIS, died 21 September, 1791, in her 35th year.

Mrs. SOPHIA DUBOIS, died 4 January, 1831, in her 59th year.

GEORGE DUBOIS, ————.

35. ———— STILLWELL, of the parish, died 7 ————, 1823.

36. LUCY, wife of JOSEPH TODD, of the parish, died 4 March, 1798, in her 31st year.

37. Rev. FREDERICK WILLIAM BLOMBERG, D.D., many years vicar of the parish, died 23 March, 1847.

38. THOMAS ————, of the parish, died 13 October, 170—, in his 53rd year.

39 CHARLOTTE, wife of JOHN ————, of the parish, died ————, aged 26.

40. ANN, wife of HENRY KNIGHT, of the parish, died 6 July 1799, aged 82.

41. HENRY BANNER, Common Council man of the ward, died 5 August, 1784, in his 49th year.

42. Family vault of WILLIAM TURNER, of Barbican, 1813.

43. Family vault of JOHN SIMKIN, of the parish, 1813.

44 SUSANNAH, wife of ROBERT WILLIAMS, died 14 ————, aged 7—.

45 Family grave of MATTHEW ELWALL.

Headstones.

46. GEORGE RYCROFT, died — November, 1822, aged 73.

GEORGE PRICE, his grandson, died 16 June, 1822, aged 7 months.

JAMES RYCROFT PRICE, died 5 October, 1824, aged 2.

47. ELIZABETH, wife of JOHN WELLS, of the parish, died 20 January, 1787, aged 28.

JOHN WELLS, their son, died at sea 21 May, 1795, aged 21.

JANE, second wife of above JOHN WELLS, died 1
April, 1799, aged 38

JOSEPH, son of JOHN and ELIZABETH WELLS, died
— March, 1702.

JOHN WELLS above, died ————, 180—.

48. THOMAS DIXON, son of JOSEPH and SARAH DIXON,
died 8 March, 1822, aged 43.

SARAH DIXON above, died 13 October, 1828, aged 78.

Mrs. SARAH CLARK, daughter of THOMAS DIXON
above, died 16 February, 1837, in her 26th year.

JOSEPH DIXON above, died — ————, ——.

49. CHARLES, son of ———— and ELIZABETH SAVAGE, of
the parish, died 23 March, 1805, aged 3 years
16 months.

MARY ANN SAVAGE, daughter of above, died 14
November, 1812, aged 13 years 4 months.

50. ANN, wife of JOHN BUCKOKE, of the parish, died
6 February, 182—, aged 57.

JOHN BUCKOKE, above, died 27 September, 183—.

51. WILLIAM GROOT, of Biggleswade, co. Bedford, died
10 December, 1785, in his 21st year.

JOHN GROOT, of same place, died 13 November,
1796, aged 60.

Footstones.

52. W.P., 1773. E.C., 1795.

53. W.S., 1824. E S., 1832. E S., 1833.

Memorandum.—Nos. 9-45, both inclusive, appear to have
been removed from the church floor.

ST. GREGORY.

Vault in St Paul's Cathedral yard.

Mural tablets. On three stones.

1. JOHN VERINDER, died 28 October, 1807, aged 57.

Mrs. ELEANOR VERINDER, died 8 July, 1812, aged
29.

HENRY WILLIAM VERINDER, died 7 August, 1809,
aged 7 months.

John Richard Verinder, son of John Verinder
above, died 23 August, 1822, aged 28

Elizabeth Verinder, relict of John Verinder
above, died 11 February, 1829, in her 77th year.

Henry Verinder, died 5 April, 1830, aged 10
months

Henry Verinder, died 7 December, 1831, aged 8
months

Sons of John Henry and Emma Verinder, grand-
sons of Henry and the above Eleanor Verinder, great-grandsons of above John and Elizabeth Verinder.

Mary Verinder, died 15 June, 1841, aged 1 day

Henry Verinder, died 4 January, 1842, aged 8.

Also son and daughter of above John Henry and
Emma Verinder

2. Charles Wilson, died 5 January, 1739, aged 42.

3. Joseph Pomfret, 1728.

4. William Kirbey, died 3 December, 1772, aged 63

Mary, his wife, died 18 November, 1775, in her
68th year.

5. Samuel Boulton, citizen and painter, died 12
September, 1762.

6. William Chambers, died 17 March, 1762, aged 64.

7. Henry Clement and Hannah, his wife. He died
23 August, 1719, aged ————.

Coffin plates.

8. " A.B.," died 8 October, 1821, aged 57.

9. William Henry Pritchard, died 6 October, 1818,
aged 10 weeks.

10. Samuel Woodward, of Hatfield Street, Christ
Church, co. Surrey, died 11 July, 1817, aged 73.

11. Elizabeth Maria Fletcher, died 17 March, 1829,
aged 18.

12. Elizabeth Fletcher, widow, died 13 April, 1839,
aged 61.

13. Mary Ann Sturges, widow, died 26 August, 1844,
aged 40

Altar tomb

14. JOHN LEWIS, died 13 June, 1788, aged 57.

 SARAH, his wife, died 28 November, 1784, aged 41.

 GEORGE, their son, died 15 November, 1771, aged 1.

 HARRIET, their daughter, died 22 April, 1772, aged 1.

 CHARLES, their son, died 20 December, 1779, aged 3.

Flat stones.

15. Rev. SAMUEL NEALE, B A., of Leicester, died 31 December, 1812, aged 25.

 JAMES NEALE, his father, died 8 February, 1814, aged 74.

16. BENJAMIN, son of JAMES NEALE, born 9 January, 1786, died 6 August, 1816

 ELIZABETH NEALE, relict of JAMES NEALE, died 5 December, 1818, aged 75.

17. HENRY TRUBEY, died 11 October, 1723, in his 27th year.

 RICHARD TRUBEY, died 25 May, 1730, in his 61st year.

18. ROBERT WILLIS, of the parish, pastry cook, died 11 August, 1765, aged 63

 ANN, wife of ROBERT WILLIS, of St. Paul's Church-yard, died 26 July, 1763, aged 47.

 Mrs. ELIZABETH FARRIN, sister-in-law to ROBERT WILLIS, of the parish, died 20 April, 1763, aged 43.

19. ELIZABETH, wife of JOHN SEARLE, died 9 June, 1740, aged 48

 THOMAS MERRIMAN, died 24 May, 1784, aged 49.

 CATHERINE, wife of H B ELLBECK, of Rotherhithe, and daughter of above, died 15 February, 1821, aged 45.

20. ELIZABETH GRIMSTEAD, died 11 December, 1740, aged 42.

 VALENTINE GRIMSTEAD, her husband, died 4 April, 1750, aged 57.

 ELEANOR SARAH, daughter of THOMAS and ELEANOR GRIMSTEAD, born 14 January, 1756, buried 6 February, 1756.

 MAY, daughter of same, born 24 October, 1759, buried 26 February, 1763.

21. JOSEPH GRIMSTEAD, of the parish, died 10 October, 1719, aged 67.
22. ELIZABETH, wife of JOHN TODD, of St. Paul's Churchyard, died 24 April, 1815, aged 54.

  JAMES TODD, son of above, died 9 November, 1806, aged 6.

  JOHN TODD above, died 22 February, 1825, **aged 70.**
23. WILLIAM KIRBEY, 1772.
24. URSULA, daughter of NATHANIEL NASH, died 12 February, 1744, aged 3.

  URSULA, wife of said NATHANIEL, died 24 May, 1759, aged 49.

  Sir NATHANIEL NASH, Knt., died 28 August, 1769, aged 68.
25. FRANCES, wife of WILLIAM HUNT, of the parish, died 14 June, 1748.

  WILLIAM HUNT, Deputy of the Ward, died 16 May, 1750, aged 52.
26. THOMAS ELLIOTT, of Blackwell Hall, Factor, died 21 March, 1748, aged 60.

  JOHN ELLIOTT, of Binfield, Berks, died 23 January, 1788.

  Mrs. HANNAH ELLIOTT, died 22 April, 1792, aged 68.

On the pillars.
27. Mrs. MARY PROCTOR, of 78, St. Paul's Churchyard, died 8 February, 1853, aged 45.
28. Mrs ELIZABETH ANN WILLIAMS, died 23 December, 1819, aged 5—.
29. RICHARD SIMPSON, died 13 May, 1718.

ST. HELEN, BISHOPSGATE.
Ground in front of the Church.

Altar tombs.
1. GEORGE LOW, upwards of 60 years of the parish, died 13 June, 1783, aged 69.

  MARY, his wife, died 1 February, 1761, aged 37.

  Five of their children who died infants.

Two children of GEORGE Low above, by a second marriage.

GEORGE ARCHDALE Low, late of Joiners' Hall, Upper Thames Street, Packer, son of GEORGE Low above, died 3 August, 1816, in his 61ʳᵗ year.

Captain THOMAS LOW, formerly of 2nd Regiment Life Guards, youngest son of GEORGE Low above, died 2 August, 1850, aged 78

JANE, his wife, only daughter of JAMES JARDINE, formerly Provost of Dumfries, died 12 February, 1851, aged 80.

Mrs. ELIZABETH HOUSTON, wife of THOMAS HOUSTON, of the parish, died ———, 1788, aged 59.

THOMAS HOUSTON above, — November, 1796, aged 61.

MARGARET, wife of SAMUEL HOUSTON, son of THOMAS and ELIZABETH HOUSTON above, died ———— 18—, aged 68.

Arms—(Arg.) on a bend (gu.) three lioncels pass. (or) for *Lem.*

JOSEPH LEM, Citizen of London, died 21 August, 1686, in his —6 year, had issue by his first wife DEBORAH 1 son and 4 daughters, and by ANN, second wife, 2 sons and 9 daughters, of which 16, 11 died young. The 5 surviving were DEBORAH by first wife, and ELIZABETH, JOSEPH, MARY and ANN, by ANN, his relict

ANN LEM, relict of JOSEPH above, died — November, 1701, in her —6ᵗʰ year.

ANN, daughter of JOSEPH and ANN LEM, died 12 March, 1707, in her —6ᵗʰ year.

ELIZABETH, relict of HENRY SPURSTOWE, daughter of JOSEPH and ANN LEM, died — November, 1709, in her 40ᵗʰ year.

MARY CLAPHAM, daughter of WILLIAM CLAPHAM, of Lenham, co. Kent, by MARY his wife, daughter of JOSEPH and ANN LEM, died 21 June, 1712.

JOSEPH LEM, only surviving son of JOSEPH and ANN LEM, died — August, 1727, in his 56ᵗʰ year

Flatstone.

3. ROBERT DINGLEY, died 30 March, 1747, aged 63.

    CHARLES EDWARD SOLLY, died 2 January, 18—,
    aged 4 months.

    ABRAHAM ALFRED ARDLEY, died 27 May, 1837,
    aged 3 years 4 months.

    SUSAN ELIZABETH, wife of ANTHONY THACK—, died
    7 September, 181—, aged 68.

Headstone

4. MARY, wife of JOHN FREEMAN, died 4 August, 1831,
    aged 72.

    THOMAS EDWARDS, son-in-law of above, died
    2 November, 1830, aged 31.

    JOHN FREEMAN, above, 48 years of the parish ——.

ST. JAMES, DUKE PLACE.

Site of the Church which has been demolished

Headstones.

1. EDWARD HOLMES, of St. Leonard, Foster Lane,
    died ————, 1780, aged 60.

2. ELEANOR, wife of —— ROBERTS, died 4 January,
    1841, aged 33.

    HENRY GEORGE ROBERTS, died 31 August, 1839,
    aged 5.

    HENRY GEORGE ROBERTS, fourth son of above, died
    26 February, 1841, aged 1 year.

    EDWARD DENBY ROBERTS, fifth son of above, died
    21 April, 1841, aged 2.

    ELEANOR DENBY ROBERTS, only daughter of above,
    died [11 ?] December, 184[4 ?], aged 15 months.

    EDWARD KEEVIL ROBERTS, son of above, died ——.

Tablet.

3. SOLOMON RAINS, Sub-Treasurer to the Social Union,
    died 1864, aged 41.

ST. JAMES, GARLICK HILL.

Ground around the Church.

Headstones.

1. PETER HORNE, died 1 July, 1840, aged 66.
   PETER, his son, died 17 August, 1833, aged 37.
2. M. A. METCALF, died 28 February, 1844, aged 17.

ST. JOHN THE EVANGELIST, WATLING STREET

Site of the church which was destroyed by the Great Fire of 1666.

Mural tablets.

1. JOSEPH BELL, of the parish, died 11 March, 1801, aged 73.
   Mrs. REBECCA COLE, his daughter, died 26 July, 1791, aged 26.
   Mrs. ELIZABETH BELL, his wife, died 20 March, 1805, aged 82.
   JOSEPH BELL, of Islington, son of above, died at Tunbridge, Kent, 15 May, 1837, in his 75th year.
   CHARLES BELL, son of last, died 29 January, 1795, aged 2.
   HENRY BELL, aged 2 ⎱ both died 6 De-
   MARY ANN BELL, aged 3 months⎰ cember, 1799.
   HENRY BELL, son of JOSEPH, died 7 February, 1811, in his 32nd year.
   ELIZABETH, wife of above JOSEPH, died 20 March, 1819, in her 81st year.
2. HENRY CHASE, of Fulham, died 29 April, 1823, aged 34.
   HENRY JOHN CHASE, his son, died 22 May, 1818, aged 2 years 6 months.
3. BARNARD DAVIES HABGOOD, of the parish, died 8 January, 1826, aged 27.
   Seven of his brothers and sisters who died infants.
   Mrs. DOROTHY PERKINS. his grandmother, died 10 April, 1805, aged 68.

ST. JOHN UPON WALBROOK.

Site of the Church which was destroyed in the Great Fire
of 1666.

Altar tombs.

1. ELIZABETH, wife of HEZEKIAH WALKER, Citizen and
   Plumber, died — November, 1732.

   HEZEKIAH, their son, died — April, 1738, aged 23.

   HEZEKIAH WALKER above, died 16 March, 1748/9,
   aged 67.

   ELIZABETH, wife of HEZEKIAH WALKER, of Berk-
   hamsted St Peter, co. Hertford, died 24 July,
   1761, aged 50.

2. *Crest*—(Three ears of wheat) two in saltire and one
   in pale (or) enfiled with a ducal coronet (or) for
   Drinkwater.

   Arms—Per pale (gu and az.) on a fess wavy arg.
   between 3 garbs (or) as many billets (of the 2nd)
   for *Drinkwater*, of co. Lanc.

   WILLIAM DRINKWATER, Citizen and Grocer of
   London, died — ———, ——.

Mural tablet.

3. JOHN WILKINSON, died 8 July, 1804, aged 45 (or 15).
   URIAH WILKINSON, died 21 December, 1806, aged 45.

ST. JOHN ZACHARY.

Site of the Church which was destroyed in the Great Fire
of 1666.

Flat stones.

1. ELLEN, wife of WILLIAM WATSON, of the parish,
   died 15 June, 1826, aged 29.

   WILLIAM DORSETT, her father, died 11 April, 1827,
   aged 71.

   WILLIAM WATSON, died 27 January, 1828, aged 2
   years 11 months.

   Mrs. ELLEN DORSETT, died 10 November, 1830,
   aged 82

ADA WATSON, died 19 February, 1837, aged 15 months 3 weeks.

2. JAMES WILLIAM ————, died 19 January, 1744, —

3 RALPH COSTER DEW, died 25 October, 1812, aged 40.

ST LAWRENCE POUNTNEY.

Site of the Church which was destroyed in the great fire of 1666 and ground near by.

Altar tombs

1 ELIZABETH, wife of JOSEPH BUTTERWORTH, of St. Mary Abchurch parish, died 21 July, 1779, aged 49.

JOSEPH BUTTERWORTH above, died 9 June, 1782, in his 69th year.

2. THOMAS ASHBURNER, of Lawrence Pountney Lane, died 24 October, 1747, aged 47.

DOROTHY ASHBURNER, his wife, of Cannon Street, died 8 September, 1765, aged 57.

JOHN BUTTERWORTH, died 5 November, 1772, aged 3 years 4 months.

Ground purchased and tomb erected by JOSEPH BUTTERWORTH, of Cannon Street, who married ELIZABETH, daughter of THOMAS and DOROTHY ASHBURNER above

3. MARY ASHBURNER, daughter of WILLIAM and MARY ASHBURNER, of Bombay, died 29 December, 1777, aged 67.

Flat stones.

4 MARY BORRADAILE, widow of JOHN BORRADAILE, late of Wigton, co. Cumberland, died 11 January, 1794, aged 68.

ANN, wife of HENRY BORRADAILE, died 12 February, 1821, aged 57

HENRY BORRADAILE, son of MARY above, died 20 January, 1822, aged 62

5. ANN, wife of WILLIAM BORRADAILE, of Streatham, co. Surrey, died 1 July, 1817, in her 43rd year.

F

WILLIAM BORRADAILE above, died 1 September, 1831, in his 81st year.

MARY SUSAN, daughter of ABRAHAM and ELIZABETH BORRADAILE, died 15 July, 1817, aged 4 months.

WILLIAM PULLEN, son of JOHN WATSON and ANN STEVENS BORRADAILE, died 9 May, 1835, in his 9th year.

EMMA, daughter of Major AB——— HAWKES and MARY ANN his wife, died 10 September, 1841, in her 21st year.

The three last named were all grandchildren of WILLIAM and ANN BORRADAILE above.

6   FRANCES, wife of SAMUEL KENYON, died 7 January, 1786, aged 27, widow of JOHN LANGTON, and daughter of JOHN and MARY BORRADAILE, of Wigton, co. Cumberland.

7   CHARLOTTE, second daughter of RICHARDSON and ELIZABETH BORRADAILE, died 19 April, 1807, aged 14

ELIZABETH, eldest daughter of same, and wife of ABRAHAM BORRADAILE their nephew, born 2 June, 1790, died 2 December, 1834

ALFRED OSMOTHERLEY BORRADAILE, youngest son of ABRAHAM and ELIZABETH BORRADAILE, born 29 October, 1821, died 9 June, 1833.

8   MARY, wife of SAMUEL STEYART, of the parish, died 17 September, 1750, in her 72nd year.

Five of their children died young.

MARY STEYART, their daughter, died 11 August, 1705, in her 47th year.

SAMUEL STEYART, above, died 28 February, 1759, in his 81st year.

9.   Mrs. ANN KELLINGTON, died 26 May, 1784, aged 71, daughter of ADRIAN BEYER, of London, Merchant, whose widow built the vault.

Inscription cut by her friends Rev. Edward Davies and John Smilton

10.   ABRAHAM DE LA PIERRE, died 15 May, 1781, aged 57.

MARY, ELIZABETH, THOMAS, and ABRAHAM, his children, all died infants.

MARY, widow of above ABRAHAM, died 2 March, 1798, aged 61.

11. THOMAS, son of JAMES WILLIAM BELLAMY, Rector of the parish, and MARY C——, his wife, died 19 May, 1820, aged 4.

CHARLES ——, died 23 May, 1843, aged — years.

12. *Crest*—A demi lion [or] for *Strode*.

Arms— ————————

HENRY STRODE, died — February, 16—.

ELIZABETH, his wife, died 17 July, 1686, aged 78

HENRY STRODE, died 6 May, 1704, aged 59.

SARAH HERRING, sister to last, died 21 June, 1731, aged 85

13. Mrs. MARY TOWNSON, died 20 February, 1755.

CHARLES ROGERS, born 2 August, 1711, died 2 January, 1784

WILLIAM COTTON, married CHARLOTTE, sister to last, 1 November, 1755, died 10 December, 1791, aged 59.

CHARLOTTE COTTON, his widow, born — December, 1725, died 29 January, 1795.

ST. LEONARD, FOSTER LANE.

Ground adjoining the churchyard of St. Botolph, Aldersgate.

Mural tablet.

1. Mrs. LYDIA LUKE, died 28 November 1810, aged 41.

WILLIAM EDWARD LUKE, her son, died 14 December, 1811, aged 22.

Flat stones

2. WILLIAM RUDGE, of the parish, died 13 July, 1825, in his 28th year

JOSEPH RUDGE, his brother, died ———— 18—9, in his 40th year.

3. ANTHONY POOLE, Ironmonger, eldest son of MICHAEL POOLE, of Chesterfield, co. Derby, died 12 September, 1679, aged 36.

LIDIA, his wife, daughter of DANIEL P——, who dwelt in the parish 57 years

ST. MARGARET, LOTHBURY.

Ground around the Church

Flat stones.

1. EDWARD SPARKE, Rector of the parish,* died 13 September 1693, aged 87.

2. Mrs. JANE COLKETT, wife of D. COLKETT, ————
Six of her children ————, HENRY, ALEXANDER, HARRIET, FRANCES and ELIZABETH died infants
FRANCIS COLKETT, her son, died 20 May, 1789, aged 4 years 4 months

ST. MARGARET PATTENS.

Ground in Fen Court, Fenchurch Street.

Altar tombs

1. AMBROSE WESTON, of Fenchurch Street, died 28 January, 1810, aged 55.
MARY, his wife, died 30 November, 1811, aged 50
WILLIAM STILES, their son, died 12 November, 1807, aged 17.
LYDIA, wife of AMBROSE WESTON, of Highbury Place, son of AMBROSE and MARY above, died 26 May, 1834, aged 34.
JAMES WESTON, of Fenchurch Street and Upper Homerton, Middlesex, died 29 January, 1823, aged 62.
JANE, his wife, died 4 February, 1833, aged 67.

2. Vault built 1762 by Mrs ANNE COTESWORTH, born in the parish
Arms—Quarterly 1 and 4, ——— 3 bars ——— for ———
2 and 3, ——— a cross fleurie ——— between 4 mullets — for ———

Mural tablet

3. JOHN GOULD, died 30 May, 1798, aged 47.

---

* Rector of St. Martin, Pomeroy, 1639-1661. This stone was originally probably at St. Olave's, Old Jewry, to which St Martin was annexed after the Great Fire. A few years ago these parishes were annexed to St Margaret.

ELIZABETH GOULD, his wife, died 25 May, 1836, aged 81

JOHN, their son, died 23 June, 1857, aged 55.

ELIZABETH GOULD, daughter of above died 18 May, 1838.

Headstone.

4. MARTHA, wife of CHARLES SWAN, of the parish, died 16 January, 1798, aged 38

ELIZABETH SWAN, their daughter, died 14 May, 1797, aged 14 months.

MARTHA, daughter of above, wife of THOMAS AINGER LACK, of St. George's East, died 6 September, 1815, aged 21 years 3 months.

ST. MARTIN ORGARS.
Site of the demolished Church.

Flat stones.

1 JOSEPH EATON and family removed from the church of St Michael, Crooked Lane, when demolished.

2. The WALKER Vault

ST. MARTIN OUTWICH.
Ground in Camomile Street.

Mural tablets.

1. THOMAS BODENHAM, died 15 March, 1782, aged 40.

MARY BODENHAM, his wife, died 23 October, 1810, aged 71.

2. JAMES EVANS, of the parish, died 5 August, 1837, in his 53rd year.

MARIA SUSANNA, his wife, died 6 December, 1827, in her 41st year.

Four of their children died infants.

Headstones.

3. JACOB FREDERICK SILBERSCHILDT, Colonel in service of the King of Denmark, born 1762, died 1827.

4. WILLIAM HOLT, of the parish, died 22 March, 1828, aged 67.

SARAH HOLT, his wife, died 9 January, 1832, aged 66.

ST. MARTIN VINTRY.

Site of the Church which was destroyed by the Great Fire
of 1666.

Headstone.

1. JOHN HOGG, died 2 January, 1730, aged 88.
   Also his wife and ————.

ST. MARY ALDERMANBURY.

Ground around the Church.

Mural tablet.

1. SUSANNAH SCALES, widow of JOSEPH SCALES,
   many years of Aldgate, died in the parish
   6 March, 1842, aged 71.
   EDWARD, son of ————.

Flat stone.

2. ROBERT, son of ROBERT and HARRIOTT BORRAS, of
   the parish, died 12 April, 1840, aged 3 years
   7 months

Headstone

3. MARY, wife of WILLIAM OATLEY, of the parish, died
   25 May, 1838, aged 54.

ST. MARY, ALDERMARY.

Ground around the Church.

Flat stones.

1. *Crest*—Unicorn's head erased for *Beale.*
   Arms—[Sa] on a chev. between 3 griffins' heads
   erased [arg] 5 mullets [gu] for *Beale* impaling
   [Gu] on two bars [arg] 6 mascles 3 and 3 on a
   canton [or] a lion's face [az] for *Geere*
   MARTHA, wife of JOHN BEALE, died 10 April, 1721,
   aged 40 years 9 months

2. *Crest*—on a wreath a beaver.
   Arms—[Arg?] on a chev. az between 3 beavers
   2 and 1, 3— impaling quarterly 1 and 3 sa. a
   chev. arg. between 3 axes 2 and 1, 2 and 4, sa
   an arrow head —.

Mrs. ANNA CATHERINA SCHNEIDER, died 15 June, 1798, at 6.30 p.m., aged 57 years 3 months and 9 days.

JOHN HENRY SCHNEIDER, her husband, died 6 October, 1824, in his 82nd year.

3   *Crest*—on a wreath a [hawk] with wings expanded [arg.] beaked and belled [or] [with a string flotant from the bells gu.] for *Bell.*

Arms—[Sa] 3 bells [arg.] alternated with 3 estoiles [or] 1 and 2 for *Bell* of cos. Bucks and Berks.

Mrs. DOROTHY BELL, died 24 December, 1751, aged 60.

JOHN BELL, died 8 August, 1752, aged 66.

Mrs. ELIZABETH STUMP, died 7 March, 1754, aged 35 years.

4.   JOHN LANGMORE, died 17 January, 1769, in his 60th year.

ELIZABETH, his wife, died 16 January, 1795, aged 84.

5.   *Arms*—A fleur de lis dimidiates an open right hand — for ————

Mrs. ANN HEINEKEN, died 12 December, 1753, aged 78.

Miss MARY ANN HEINEKEN, died 11 July, 1754, aged 10 months.

FREDERICK HERMAN HEINEKEN, died 5 February, 1760, aged 76.

HERMAN HEINEKEN, M.D., died 26 June, 1772, aged 57.

Mrs. MARY ANN HUGHES, daughter of last, died 22 December, 1791, aged 36.

SAMUEL, son of last and ROBERT HUGHES, died 28 January, 1811, aged 27.

6.   RICHARD WRIGHT, died 10 June, 1752, in his 50th year.

7.   Mrs. MARGARET FRYER, died 1 October, 1728, in her 65th year.

Also three of her children.

Mrs. ELIZABETH WAILL, daughter of above, and Mr. ISAAC FRYER, of St. Thomas Apostle parish, died 4 ————, 1738.

8. ANN, wife of EDMUND SAWTEL, by whom she had 9 sons and 6 daughters, died 20 December, 1694, in her 45th year.

   JEREMIAH, their son, died 8 April, 1691, in his 24th year.

   HESTER, their daughter, died 28 December, 1694, in her 4th year.

9 JOHN KENSINGTON, of St. Thomas Apostle parish, died 22 July, 1794, aged 67.

   HENRY KENSINGTON, his youngest son, died 13 July, 1817, aged 39

10. ———— died 8 January, ——, aged 1 year 9 months.

    DAVID GRIFFITHS, died 20 January, 1822, aged 22.

    JOHN GRIFFITHS, his brother, died 23 May, 1831.

    PETER GRIFFITHS, their father, died 23 December, 1831, aged 74

    MARGARET GRIFFITHS, his wife, died ————

11 MARY, wife of THOMAS ASHWELL, died — February, 1798.

    STEPHEN, SARAH, and THOMAS, their children, who died infants.

12 PERCIVALL POTTS, F R.S., died 22 December, 1788, aged 75.

    Mrs. SARAH FRYE, his eldest daughter, died 27 October, 1791, aged 41

    Mrs. MARY LITCHFIELD, eldest daughter of J. R. FRYE, and above SARAH and wife of H. C. LITCHFIELD, died 22 January, 1806, aged 31.

    Mrs SARAH POTT, relict of above, died 18 January, 1811, aged 87.

    Miss MARY LITCHFIELD, second daughter of RICHARD LITCHFIELD, of Torrington, co. Devon, died 1 March, 1811, aged 27.

    PERCIVALL POTT, eldest son of above PERCIVALL, died 27 January, 1833, aged 83.

    SARAH FRYE, daughter of J. R. FRYE and granddaughter of PERCIVALL POTT, senr., died 9 March, 1844, aged 69.

Ven. JOSEPH HOLDEN POTT, M.A., Chancellor
of Exeter, and late Archdeacon of London,
died 17 February, 1847, aged 88

13 JOHN SEALE, of London, Merchant, died 11 July,
1715, in his 48th year.

14 JANE, wife of RALPH DARVILL, of the parish, died
————, aged 5— years.
Above RALPH DARVILL, died 14 September, 1760,
aged 61.
MARGARET MARIA DARVILL, died ————.

15 WILLIAM LOVEDAY, born 2— October, 166—, died
2 April 1671.
JOHN LOVEDAY, born 27 January, 1669, died
20 April 1670.
The two children of WILLIAM LOVEDAY.

16. Sir JOHN SMITH, Knt., Alderman and Sheriff of
London, son of JAMES SMITH, of Friday Street.
First married to ANN, daughter of WILLIAM
WAYES, of Windsor, by whom he had one son
survive, and secondly to JANE, daughter of
ROBERT DEAN, of the parish, by whom he had
six sons and three daughters, three sons and
two daughters surviving Died 17 June, 1673,
aged 46.

Inscribed beneath to the effect that the altar piece
of this Church and the rails and frame of the
Communion table were the gift of Dame JANE
SMITH, relict of Sir JOHN SMITH.

17. MARY, relict of JOHN HARRINGTON, died 29 Decem-
ber, 1796.
ESTHER MACKETT, died 10 December, 1798, aged
60.
JOHN THOMAS HARRINGTON, son of JOHN and
ESTHER H., died 21 December, 1804, aged 3
JOHN, son of above MARY, died 28 May, 1814,
aged 68.

18 JANE, wife of RICHARD BORD, of Watling Street,
born 13 April, 1793, died 8 January, 1839.

RICHARD BORD, a servant of the Bank of England, died at Bruton, co. Somerset his native place, 29 ———, 1848, in his 57th year.

19. HONORIUS COMBAULD, of St. Thomas Apostle, died 26 March, 178—, aged 67.

HONORIUS COMBAULD, his eldest son, died 23 September, 1803, aged 50.

Mrs. MARGARET COMBAULD, wife of the first, and mother of the second, died 23 April, 182—, aged 89.

20. GEORGE BLAGDEN, died 6 February, 1795, aged 45.

ROBERT DRUCE, died 20 August, 1800, aged 7[0?].

Mrs. ANN DRUCE, widow of last, died 27 December, 1804, aged 88

Mrs. SARAH VINCENT DRUCE, daughter-in-law of last, died 26 March, 1811, aged 55.

21. PETER WRIGHT, died 13 January, 1765, aged 57.

CATHERINE WRIGHT, his wife, died 30 January, 1798, aged 81.

PETER WRIGHT, eldest son of above, died 24 September, 1806, aged 67

Mrs. HANNAH WELDON, daughter of PETER and CATHERINE WRIGHT, born 1736, died 1811.

JAMES WELDON, her husband, ———, 1817.

——— WRIGHT ———.

22. WILLIAM REYNOLDS, Wine Merchant and Deputy of the Ward, died 8 January, 1756, in his 58th year.

23. Mrs. SUSANNA EDELMAN, died 2 January, 1812, aged 53.

Mr. JOHN CHRISTOPHER EDELMAN, died 28 January, 1817, aged 62

MARY, daughter of JOHN FREDERIC and ELIZABETH FIXSEN, grand-daughter of above, died 12 January, 1833, aged 13

24. ——— died 5 July, 1756, aged 63.

Mrs. ELEANOR BROMLEY, his wife, died 12 January, 1739/40, aged 38.

25. SAMUEL ROBINSON, died 13 February, 1797, aged 65.

ELIZABETH ROBINSON, his wife, died 17 March, ———, in her 86th year

26. Mrs ANNA MARIA COXE, wife of EDWARD COXE, died 25 July, 1787, aged 36.

27. JOHN ABRAHAMS, died — September, ————, aged 77. All the above appear to have been originally in the floor of the Church. No. 16 was before the rail of the Communion Table.

Head stones.

28. THOMAS HILL, son of ———— ————INGTHORP JOHN (PALMER?) of B————, in the parish, died 19 November, 1773, in his 37th year

29. C. F. LOUDONSACK, died 5 March, 1802, aged 66 WILLIAM WIDDERS, died 12 October, 1807, aged 56. ALICE LOUDONSACK, wife of C. F. LOUDONSACK, died 31 October, 1809, aged 65.

   F. W. LOUDONSACK, son of C. F. and A. LOUDONSACK, died ————

30. MARY, wife of WILLIAM COUTHIT, died 29 January, 1775, aged 43.

   Above named WILLIAM died 18 February, 1808, aged 63.

   ELIZABETH COUTHIT, died ————.

ST. MARY-AT-HILL.

Ground North of the Church

Flatstone.

1. THOMAS PERRY, died 3 June, 1825, aged 61 MARY, his wife, died 19 March, 1846, aged 7— Many years inhabitants of Eastcheap, parish of St. Andrew Hubbard

   Also their children :—

   MARY ANNE, died 25 January, 1802, aged 2 years 6 months

   RICHARD WILLIAM, ————

   WILLIAM HENRY ————

Headstones

2. SARAH KNIGHT, daughter of THOMAS and SARAH KNIGHT, died 17 September, 1772, aged 3 years 9 months.

3. EDWARD BODENHAM, died 12 August, 1840, aged 45.
EDWARD, his son, died 1 May, 1830, aged 11 months.
MARTHA, his daughter, died 1 December, 1835, aged 8 months
EDWARD, his second son, died 25 March, 1838, aged 14 months

4. SARAH SLATER VICKERS, daughter of WILLIAM HENRY and CHARLOTTE STORER VICKERS, of the parish, died 8 June, 1831, aged 2 years 1 month.
JOHN DAVYS VICKERS, son of above, died 5 May, 1844, aged 6 years 9 months.

ST. MARY, SOMERSET.

Site of the Church demolished

Flat stones apparently removed from the interior of the Church

1. ELIZABETH, wife of WILLIAM GRAHAM, of the parish, died 9 June, 1803, aged 47.
WILLIAM GRAHAM, above, died 22 October, 1821, aged 69.
RICHARD PARTON, of Trig Lane, died 10 October, 1834, aged 65.

2. ELIZABETH MARGARET GRAHAM, daughter of WILLIAM and ELIZABETH GRAHAM, of the parish, died 9 February, 1805, aged 21
GRAHAM LINDSAY, daughter of JAMES LINDSAY, late merchant in Glasgow, and KATHERINE INNES his wife, daughter of Rev. HUGH INNES, all deceased, died 27 November, 1806, aged 27.
Rev JOHN GRAHAM, Vicar of Windsor, died 28 April, ——, aged 35
JANE, eldest daughter of WILLIAM and ELIZABETH GRAHAM, wife of JOSEPH WILLMORE,. died — March, 1839, in her 61st year

3. CHARLES CHURCH, died — May, 1804, aged 2 years 5 months.
ALFRED CHURCH, died — May, 1804, aged 5 months,

———— Church, died — December, 1809, aged
10 months.

Thomas Church, their father, died ————

4. John Toolye, Deputy of the Ward, died 2 July,
1714, aged 78.

Richard Shuckburgh, of Lincoln College, Oxford,
M.A., son-in-law of above, died 28 August,
1714, aged 35.

John Toolye, ————, died 4 ————, aged 66.

5. John Chapman, of the parish, died ————, 1787,
in his 53rd year

Harriot Chapman, his youngest daughter, died
28 January, 180—, in her 21st year.

Hannah Chapman, second wife of above, died
6 February, 1810, aged 53.

Mrs. Laura Bowles, daughter of above, died 6
April, 1824, aged 55

John Chapman died 27 April, 1830, aged 63.

6. Sarah, daughter of John and Mary Ogdin, of the
parish, died 22 May, 1789, aged 4 years.

Mary Ogdin, above, died 18 March, 1808, aged 62.

John Ogdin, above, died 17 January, 1818, aged 70.

7. Ann Lamb————, wife of ————, died — January,
180—.

ST. MARY STAINING.

Site of the Church which was destroyed by the Great Fire,
1666.

Headstones.

1. Thomas Wood, son of the late John Wood,
farmer, of Chipstead, co. Surrey, died 11 August,
1838, in his 39th year

2. Sarah, wife of Thomas Wheatley, of St. Michael
Wood Street parish, died 17 June, 1709.

Three sons ————, Edward and William.

3. Mary Williams, died 14 July, 1725, aged 34.

William Williams, died 10 August, 1752, aged 70.

SARAH MERITON, their daughter, died 15 June, 1757 aged 34.

SARAH, daughter of above ————.

4. ELIZABETH, wife of THOMAS PAGE, citizen and butcher, of Leadenhall Market, died ————, 1758, aged 44.

5. *Arms*—(Gu.) on a fess (erm.) between 3 annulets (or) a lion pass. (az) in chief a cross crosslet fitchée between 2 annulets (arg.) for *Underwood* of London.

JOHN UNDERWOOD, many years Deputy of the Ward, died ————.

6. GEORGE TATTERSALL, died 12 July, 1847, aged 48.

7. Miss MARY BAWTREY, of the parish, died 14 April, 1803, aged 57

8. MARY ABDY, died 10 January, 1820, aged 58.

9. RICHARD THOMAS HOPKINS, of the parish, died 6 July, 1803, aged 56.

ELIZABETH HOPKINS, his wife, died 5 March, 1805, aged 62.

CLARISSA ANN ST————, their daughter, died 7 January, 1822, aged 46.

SARAH COLSON, daughter of above, died 16 May, 1836, aged 57.

WILLIAM COLSON, died 14 March, 1843, aged 55.

ST. MICHAEL, PATERNOSTER ROYAL.
Ground around the Church.

Headstone.

HANS HENRY ECKEN, died 31 January, 17—3, aged 4.

ST. MICHAEL, QUEENHITHE.
Site of the Church demolished about 1875.

Mural tablet.

1. JOHN NIXON, died 19 August, 1754, aged —.

Flat stones all apparently removed from the Church floor.

2. ELIZABETH COCKERILL, died 26 August, 1769, aged 59.

   HENRY COCKERILL, died 7 June, 1782, aged 80.

3. EDWARD, son of JOHN and MARGARET ALICE SMITH, of the parish, died 9 July, 180—, aged 7.

   ANN BEDELL SMITH, their only daughter, died 14 March, 1814, in her 20th year.

   JOHN SMITH above, died 30 July, 183—, aged 80.

   WILLIAM, his son, died 7 August, 183—, aged 36.

4. JOHN, son of JOHN RANDELL, died ————.

5. MARTHA, wife of ZEBEDEE PARKER, of the parish, died 2 January, 1802, aged 61.

   ZEBEDEE PARKER, an ancient inhabitant of the parish, died 30 June, 1806, in his 65th year.

   FRANCES, wife of JOHN DEPCKE, of the parish of St. Saviour's, Southwark, died 5 February, 1812, aged 35.

6. ROBERT MOSER, husband of ELIZABETH MOSER, of the parish, died — October, ——.

   Children who died infants.

   JOHN MOSER, died ————, 180—, aged —7.

   ROGER MOSER, nephew of last, died 5 November, 1810, aged 49.

7. WILLIAM JARVIS, of the parish, died 10 June, 1798, aged 59.

   ANN JARVIS, his wife, died 13 November, 1801, aged 59.

   RICHARD JOHN JARVIS, grandson of above, died in infancy.

   ROBERT MOORE died 21 June, 1809, aged 49.

   MARY MOORE, his wife, daughter of above, died 6 May, 1832, aged 63.

   WILLIAM, son of WILLIAM and ANN JARVIS above, died 3 May, 1833, aged 55.

   THOMAS, brother of last, died 2 August, 1834, aged 58.

   ELLIS JARVIS, died 20 May, 1842, aged 70.

   MARY, wife of WILLIAM JARVIS, died 29 September, 1847, aged 75.

8　JOHN PIPER, Citizen and Merchant Taylor of London, for several years Deputy of the Ward, died 19 December, 1777, aged 56.

　　ELIZABETH PIPER, his widow, died 29 January, 1795, aged 66.

9　Master FREDERIC BEACHCROFT, died 30 April, 1804.

　　Miss CHARLOTTE BEACHCROFT, died 27 February, 1808.

10　WILLIAM LONG, an ancient inhabitant of Trinity parish and constant worshipper at St Michael's, died 27 January, 1807, aged 76

　　LUCY, his daughter, died 17 September, 1813, aged 36.

　　SARAH, his second daughter, died 16 March, 1814, aged 34.

　　ELLEN LONG, his widow, died 13 September, 1819. aged 76.

11　SARAH LONDON, died 22 October, 1776, aged 7 months

12.　Mrs. ELIZABETH LYON, widow of JAMES LYON, died — July, 1805

　　JAMES LYON, died 20 August, 182—, aged 53.

　　MARY LYON, his daughter, born 24 March, 1809 ; died 25 June, 1822

13.　ROBERT WILCOX, died ————, aged —4—

　　ANN WILCOX, died ————, 177—, aged 12 months.

　　JOSEPH WILCOX, brother of above, died — March, ——, aged 30.

　　THOMAS WILCOX, late of Wimbledon, co. Surrey, died — December, 1806

　　ELIZABETH WILCOX, his wife, died — March, 1832, aged 8—.

　　ISAAC ——— WILCOX, son of ———, died ———, aged — weeks.

14.　WILLIAM, son of WILLIAM and MARY SOPPITT, of the parish, died 10 February, 1789, aged 6 years, 6 months

　　WILLIAM SOPPITT, died 8 March, 1821, aged 81.

　　JAS SOPPITT, died 25 December, 1828, aged 48.

MARY SOPPITT, wife of WILLIAM, above, died 23 June, 1833, aged 81.

15. Mrs. MARY WRIGHT, ————.

16. MARY BUCKLEY, daughter of Mrs. ANN BUCKLEY, of the parish, died 29 June, 1775, aged 24.

ANN, wife of WILLIAM BESWICK, died 17 March, 178—, aged 55.

WILLIAM BESWICK, died 17 September, 1801, aged 68

17 JOANE, wife of RICHARD HOWELL, of Haverfordwest, co. Pembroke, died 28 November, 1689, in her 68th year.

MARY HOWELL, sister of RICHARD above, died 4 November, 1690, in her 58th year.

18 ROBERT ALSOP, died 24 May, 17—5, aged 78.

MARY ALSOP, his wife, died 18 November, 1786, aged 88.

19. ———— COLEMAN, died ————, 179—.

GEORGE COLEMAN, died 20 February, 1815, aged 38

20. ANN, wife of BENJAMIN SMITH, citizen and leather-seller, of the parish, died 26 November, 1788, aged 37.

21. Mrs. MARY PAYNE, died —4th December, 1796, aged (8?)4.

22. JONATHAN DOWNES, of the parish, born 21 May, 1740, died 2(5?) May, 181—.

SARAH DOWNES, his wife, born 18 January, 17—5, died 1 April ——.

MARY ————, her daughter, died ————.

23. SAMUEL CLARKE, of the parish, died 25 January, 1753, aged 57.

ANN CLARKE, died 1 April, 1758, aged 17.

ELIZABETH LEAKE, died 24 September, 17—.

24. JOHN and MARY MAYLNS family grave, 1804

25. JOHN BIGGS ————.

26. Family vault of R. P. JONES, 1827.

27. Two infant children of WILLIAM and MARY ALLEN, of Holy Trinity parish, late of Garth U——, co. Salop, viz. :—EDWARD, died — December, 1812, aged 6 months — days ; JOHN, died 17 March, 181—, aged 2 years 29 days.

ST. OLAVE, HART STREET.
Ground South of the Church.

Altar tombs.

1. JAMES WARING, son of JASPER WARING, H.M. Consul at Alicante, Spain, died 20 February, 1836. aged 21.

2. Mrs. JANE TABER, died 4 January, 1820, aged 70.

3. Children of WILLIAM and MARY RIXON, of the parish, viz.:—

    CHARLOTTE, died 15 April, 1804, aged —o months.

    EDWARD, died 18 February, 1813, aged 7 months

    HENRY, died 31 July, 1837, aged 30 years.

    JOHN SOUTER RIXON, son of WILLIAM and MARY RIXON above, died 6 December, 1839, aged 39.

    WILLIAM RIXON, died 25 April, 1851, aged 73, leaving a widow and children surviving.

Brass plate in ground.

4. Vault of DAVID EVANS, 1815.

Flat stones.

5 MARY ANN GOODHALL, died 19 November, 1838, aged 42.

6. Mrs. M. E. GOODHALL, died 25 January, 1805, aged 32.

    Mrs. ANN CHANNING, died 3 December, 1814, aged 76.

    HENRY HUMPHREY GOODHALL, born 22 January, 1766, died 3 Nov., 1835.

7. MARY, wife of JOHN BISHOP, of the parish, died 4 March, 1848, in her 76th year.

Headstones.

8 MARY ANN, wife of JAMES PAPINEAU, of the parish, died 14 June, 1824, aged 26.

    CHARLES PAPINEAU, died 18 March, 1830, aged 13 months.

    FREDERICK PAPINEAU, died 1 January, 1839, aged 8 years.

    JAMES PAPINEAU, father of above children, died 15 January, 1841, aged 51.

    SARAH PAPINEAU, wife of last, died 7 July, 1845, aged 53.

9. Mrs. ELIZABETH ALDOUS, died 1 June, 1843, aged 43.

10. SARAH, wife of JAMES CROCKER, of the parish, died 15 September, 1830, aged 31.

JAMES CROCKER, her husband, died 19 June, 1832, aged 30.

11. WILLIAM BOWLES, died 20 April, 1852, aged 64.

12. ANNE MARGARET, daughter of QUARLES and ANNE HARRIS, of Billiter Square, died 30 December, 1833, aged 11 years 9 months.

QUARLES, son of above, died 22 November, 1821, aged 6 months.

13. ROBERT GRAVES, died 6 January, 1816, aged 62.

14. JOHN FOTHERGILL, died 28 March, 1845, aged 7— years.

15. JAMES EDWARDS, of the parish, died 28 April, 1822, aged 54.

CHARLES EDWARDS, died 11 March, 1798, aged 9 months 11 days.

JAMES EDWARDS, died 17 August, 1813, aged 17 months.

GEORGE EDWARDS, died 28 February, 1815, aged 9 years.

Children of the above JAMES and SARAH, his wife.

Said Mrs. SARAH EDWARDS, died 3 August, 1828, aged 57.

16. JOSEPH HUDSON, died 3 June, 1805, aged 46.

17. Family grave of EDWIN and ISABELLA BLACKBURN, of Savage Gardens

Their children :—

MARY SOPHIA, died 12 September, 1841, aged 3 years 5 months.

WILLIAM BOWLES, died 23 December, 1850, aged 13 months.

MARGARET, died 30 December, 1850, aged 3 years 8 months.

18. MARY ANN BALLARD LAMBERT, of the parish, died 23 November, 1831, aged 36, leaving a husband and 9 children surviving.

G 2

19   HENRIETTA REBECCA, wife of JOHN EDWARD GATOR OSMOND, died 12 January, 1837, aged 27, after a long and painful illness

20.   SARAH ANN ALCHORNE, died 24 October, 1804, aged 1 year 3 months.

Footstone.

21.   T.J., 1796.   F.J., 18—0

ST. OLAVE, SILVER STREET.

Site of the Church which was destroyed in the Great Fire of 1666.

Altar tombs.

1.   Family grave of JOHN BULL.
2.   Family grave of WILLIAM KERL, of the parish.
    JAMES ———— KERL, grandson of above died — February, 1802.

ST. PAUL'S CATHEDRAL
Ground around the Cathedral.

Altar tombs

1.   ——————— EDWARD BENTLEY
    MARTHA NICHOL ————
2.   CLARISSA KING, died 21 May, 1837, in her 7th year
    LAURA, wife of WILLIAM KING in her 51st year.
3.   FRANCES, wife of BROOKES HINTON, died 9 January, 181—, aged 29
    BROOKES HINTON, above, died 7 January, 1837, aged 60.
    ANNE, wife of THOMAS JERVIS AMOS, of Kennington, died 4 June, 1837, aged 33.
    MATILDA, wife of HENRY NORTHCOTE, youngest daughter of BROOKES and FRANCES HINTON above, died 9 April, 1839, aged 31 years.
    MATILDA, youngest daughter of HENRY and MATILDA HINTON, died 23 June, 1839, aged 6 months.

4. Children of HENRY and Sarah KING ; died infants

GEORGE, son of above, died — July, 1801, aged 11 years 2 months

SARAH KING, above, died 12 January, 1809, aged 62.

HENRY KING, above, died 30 July, 1820, in his 78th year

JAMES KING, son of above, died — December, 1832, aged —9.

MARY ANN, wife of HENRY KING, of ———— House, Essex, died — June, 1839, aged —1.

Mrs. Mary ————, died 9th ——.

5. WILLIAM TRINGHAM POWELL, died ———— 1824, aged 11 months.

MARION POWELL, died 9 February, 1826, aged 1 year 4 months.

Grandchildren of JOSEPH and ANN TRINGHAM.

JOSEPH TRINGHAM, of St. John's, Wood, son of WILLIAM and ELIZABETH TRINGHAM, died 3 January, 1840, aged 82

ANN TRINGHAM, his wife, died 29 November, 1843, aged 81

Their three sons .—

CHARLES EDWARD TRINGHAM, died 2 March, 179—, aged 6 weeks

JOHN TRINGHAM, died — November ——.

JAMES TRINGHAM, died ————.

WILLIAM TRINGHAM, Esq., died 10 March ——.

ELIZABETH TRINGHAM, his wife, died — August, ——.

6. Family grave of JOHN SELBY.

———— SELBY, —— Surrey, died 16 May, 1837, aged 66.

SARAH, his wife, died 5 Oct. 1840.

7. THOMAS WILLIAM MELLER, of Denmark Hill, Surrey, died 8 April, 1850, aged 80.

8 MARY ANN, third daughter of WILLIAM JOSHUA and SARAH TILLEY, of Christ Church, Surrey, died 15 December, 1828, aged 7 years 9 months.

SARAH TILLEY, her mother, died 8 February, 1835, aged 44

JAMES HOPW——D TILLEY, son of WILLIAM JOSHUA and SARAH TILLEY.

ROB. ———, died ——— 1846.

Flat stones.

9. PHILIP CHARLES MOORE, of Doctor's Commons, born 19 August, 1805, died 21 January, 1849, son of WILLIAM MOORE, of Doctors' Commons, and MARY ANN, his wife, who with three infant children are buried in the churchyard of St. Benet, Paul's Wharf, and grandson of PHILIP and MARY MOORE, buried near this stone

CAROLINE AMELIA MOORE, daughter of PHILIP CHARLES MOORE, above, born 3 February, 1837, died 16 March, 1856.

10. PHILLIPA, daughter of PHILIP and MARY MOORE, of Doctors' Commons, died — February, 18—.

MARY MOORE, wife of PHILIP, died — March, 1807.

11. JOHN PLOWES, of Leeds, co York, died 17 June, 1812, aged 62.

12. ——— REMNANT, of the parish, died ———, 1821.

———, mother of above, died 23 January, 1828, aged 37

Mrs. ELIZABETH ———, mother of above, died 21 June, 1833, aged 72.

Mrs ELIZABETH MORGAN, died 1 February, 1837, aged 77

MARY ETHRINGTON REMNANT, sister of above, died 21 June, 1839, aged 33

JAMES REMNANT, grandson of above, died 16 October, 1839, aged 5 years, 1 month.

EMMA REMNANT, grand-daughter of above, died 10 December, 1839, aged 1 month.

SARAH REMNANT, grand-daughter of above, died 22 March, 1843, aged 10½ years.

FREDERICK REMNANT, above, died 30 May, 1853, aged 72

13. CHARLES GWINNELL, of Prerogative Office, Doctors' Commons, died 6 March, 1841, aged 73.

WILLIAM GWINNELL, of Gower Street, Bedford Square, died 16 February, 1840, aged 82.

ST. PETER, CHEAP.

Site of the Church which was destroyed in the Great Fire of 1666

Mural tablets.

1. JOHN STAPLER, died 25 March, 1810, aged 2 years, 4 months, son of J. and S. STAPLER, of Cross Key Inn, Wood Street, Cheapside.

WILLIAM STAPLER, uncle to above, died 30 April, 1810, aged 25.

CHARLES STAPLER, his brother, died 19 May, 1810, aged 22.

2. WILLIAM CANNER, Marshall of the City, died 13 January, 180[3 or 5], aged 59.

JOHN WILLIAM CANNER, his son, died 12 October, 1788, in his 19th year.

Mrs. HANNAH CANNER, died 29 December, 1808, aged 68

Headstone.

3. ANNE ROGERS, wife of THOMAS ROGERS, of the parish, died 25 November, 1791, aged 78.

OBADIAH WICKES ROGERS, their son, died 24 February, ——, aged 59.

Mrs. ANNE ROGERS, his wife, died ———, aged 78.

ST. PETER, CORNHILL.

Ground South of the Church.

Mural tablets.

1. HENRY PARRY, died 16 February, 1822, aged 43.
2. THOMAS ATKINSON, of Corbet Court, in the parish, died 8 March, 1816, aged 48.

    SARAH, JAMES and WILLIAM, his children, who died infants

    AGNES ELIZA, his fourth daughter, died 24 December, 1834, in her 22nd year.

    MARY ANN ATKINSON, his relict, died 17 June, 1836, aged 58.

3   MARY, wife of JOHN BAYLEY, formerly of the parish, died 16 March, 1811, aged 67.

    Above JOHN BAYLEY, died 18 January, 1816, aged 75.

    JOHN BAYLEY, his son, died 27 November, 1837, aged 75.

4   EDWARD DUNCAN, Surgeon of the parish, died 30 April, 1848, aged 41,

        Leaving a widow and five infant children.

5   CHARLES RANOE, died 20 March, 1839, in his 47th year.

    Erected by ANN RANOE, his daughter.

6   MARY, wife of WILLIAM GOULD, of Gracechurch Street, died 1 January, 1811, aged 67.

    WILLIAM GOULD, her husband, died 5 January, 1833, in his 89th year

    SARAH ELIZABETH GOULD, their daughter, died 4 June, 1827, aged 67.

    ANNE LYDIA, wife of THOMAS HOBSON, of Grafton Street, Fitzroy Square, died 26 January, 1827, aged 53

7   JAMES WILLIAM JEFFERISS, died 13 April, 1824, aged 45.

    MARY JEFFERISS, his relict, died 15 May, 1853, in her 73rd year.

8   SARAH, wife of CHRISTOPHER JOHN PEACOCK, of the parish, died 1 December, 1813, in her 71st year.

    Above CHRISTOPHER JOHN PEACOCK, died 9 September, 1815, aged 78

    Mrs. ELIZABETH CORK, their daughter, died 22 February, 1833, aged 67

Nos. 4, 5, 6, 7, and 8, have been repainted many times and unimportant errors have obviously crept into the lettering. It is therefore possible that the particulars abstracted cannot be relied upon

Headstones.

9. JOHN BUTLER ————.
10. THOMAS DAY, died 13 January, 1805, in his 61st year.

Mrs. RACHEL PRICE, his widow, died 29 March, 1812, in her 69th year.

CATHERINE DAY, died 26 April, 1806, aged 4 years 7 months.

WILLIAM DAY, died 2— September, 1819, aged 7 years — months.

ST. PETER, PAUL'S WHARF.

Site of the Church which was destroyed in the Great Fire of 1666.

Altar tomb

1. JOSEPH ————, died 24 June, ——, aged 6—.

Headstones

2. THOMAS WRIGHT, died 29 May, 1845, in his 62nd year, father of the late Mrs. MARY ANN BURNET.
3. CAROLINE, wife of JAMES BURNET, died 26 July, 1830, aged 36.

MARY ANN, his second wife, died 12 April, 1840, aged 36.

JAMES BURNET, above, died ————, 1842, aged —3.

4. Mrs. ANN ATKIN, of the parish, died 25 February, 1835, in her 55th year.

JOHN ATKIN, her husband, died 25 June, 1847, in his 64th year.

ST. SEPULCHRE, NEWGATE
Ground around the Church

Mural tablets.

1. CHARLES HILL, eldest son of CHARLES HILL, of West Smithfield, died 13 August, 1834, aged 29.

Mrs. ANN HILL, wife of CHARLES HILL Senr., above
died 21 January, 1837, aged 51.

CHARLES HILL, her husband, died 19 December,
1846, aged 72.

Mrs. ANN AUSTIN, daughter of above, died 23
February, 1852, aged 41.

2. ROBERT POPE, painter, died 22 December, 1768, in
his 65th year.

3. RICHARD COCHER, died 15 September, 1819, aged
43.

Altar tomb.

4. SARAH, wife of EDWARD CHANDLER, Senr., many
years of this parish, died 29 April, 1779, in her
68th year.

Five of their grandchildren.

EDWARD CHANDLER, died 2 October, 1781, aged 70.

EDWARD CHANDLER, Junr., died 17 February, 1780,
aged 37

EDWARD CHANDLER, son of last, died 17 May, 1824,
in his 56th year

ANN CHANDLER, wife of last, died 5 June, 1841,
aged 67

EDWARD CHANDLER, son of last, died 18 July, 1840,
aged 40.

JOHN SPICER FISHER, died 2 May, 1846, aged 76

NANCY FISHER, his wife, died 5 November, 1837,
aged 63.

MATILDA CHANDLER, their daughter, died 28
August, 1842, aged 3—.

Flat stones.

5. THOMAS CARPENTER, died 24 February, 1833,
aged 52.

ELEANOR, his wife, died 1 June, 1839, in her 57th year.

6. JOHN CLARK, of the parish, died 7 July, 1835, in
his 66th year.

SARAH, his wife, died 25 August, 1840, in her
72nd year.

HENRY RICHARD CLARK, their son, died 20 March,
1836, aged 58.

GEORGE ALFRED HANCOCK, their grandson, died 23 August, 1848, in his 21ˢᵗ year.

Their grandchildren :—

GEORGIANA BEST, died — October, 183[6 or 0], in her 2ⁿᵈ year.

EDGAR HANCOCK, died 18 November, 1837, in his 3ʳᵈ year.

THOMAS DINGEY BEST, died ————,

CHARLES HANCOCK, died ————, 1842

7. AMELIA BURCHELD. ⁚

ST. STEPHEN, COLEMAN STREET.
Ground around the Church

Flat stones.

1. Date " 1685 " legible only

2. SOPHIA —AMBEL GROOMBRIDG, died — October, —— aged 33.

    JOHN GROOMBRIDG, her husband, organist.

    ———— mother of SOPHIA, above, died 1 November, 1831, aged 82.

3. JOHN RICHARDS, of London, merchant, died 11 April, 1769, in his ——ty-third year.

    JOHN RICHARDS, merchant, his nephew, died — August, 1730, in his 29ᵗʰ year.

    DOROTHY, daughter of ————, of Edmonton, co. Middlesex.

4. *Arms*—[Arg] on a chev [gu.] 3 [bezants] for *Bromley* impaling — on a fess — between 3 [bulls?] heads erased — 3 [bezants] for ————.

    ELIZABETH, wife of JONATHAN BROMLEY, of the parish, she had seven sons and two daughters, died 1 February.

    JONATHAN BROMLEY, above, Citizen and Fishmonger of London, died 14 February, 1739, aged 54

5. JOHN FREEMAN, Merchant of London, died 31 January, ——, aged 66

6. *Arms*—— a fess — between 3 daggers — for ——

    RICHARD TREANGE (or TREANGT), of the parish, died — December, 1741, aged 63.

7. Mrs. ANN LOCKE, died 18 November, 1795, last
surviving daughter of RICHARD and BRIDGET
LOCKE, buried near by

Mrs. MARY LOCKE, daughter of WALTER and MARY
LOCKE, and neice of above, died 20 September,
1824, aged 76.

8. JULIA STEWART KERSHAW died 1 January, 1824,
aged 5 months.

9. *Crest*—[A tiger's?] head erased [sa.] for *Lingard.*
Arms— — 2 bars — a bend — for *Lingard,*
impaling —

JOHN LINGARD, Common Serjeant of the City, one of
the Common Pleaders and one of the Judges of
the Sheriffs' Court, married SARAH, daughter of
JAMES RICHARDSON, Citizen and Haberdasher,
and SARAH, his wife), with whom he spent 25
years, and had children surviving, viz · ELIZA-
BETH, SARAH, ANNE, FRANCES. Died 4 November, 1729, in his 54th year.

Headstones

10 LYDIA, wife of RICHARD READ, of the parish, died
14 May, 1784, aged 57

DAVID WOODHAM, nephew of above, died 12 May,
1784, aged 15

RICHARD READ, above, died 27 March, 1793,
aged 59.

11. WILLIAM ARTHUR MARTIN, died 3 January, 18—, in
his 4th year

12. GEORGE KEY, of Mile End Road, died 23 February,
1838, aged 66.

13. CHARLES ——— HILL, died 27 May, ——, aged
(3 or 5) 5.

————, died — December, aged 32.

ST. STEPHEN'S, WALBROOK.
Ground East of the Church.

Flat stones

1. ROBERT ROYDS, died 30 January, 1780, aged 58.

JEREMIAH ROYDS, died 27 August, 1796, aged 45

2. JOSEPH WILLIAMS, of the parish, died 9 January, 1716, in his 44th year.

3. BENJAMIN TORIN, of Englefield Green, Surrey, died 15 August, 1784, aged 62

    MARY ANN TORIN, his youngest daughter, died 19 March, 1792, aged 16

    CHARLES BEAUVOIR TORIN, youngest son of above, died 25 January, 1803, aged 29

    BENJAMIN TORIN, grandson of above, died 1 December, 1812, aged 7.

    Mrs. ANNE TORIN, wife of above BENJAMIN TORIN, died 3 September, 1821, aged 87

    CHARLES WEST, died 15 February, 1799, in his 60th year.

    ELEANOR, wife of JOHN GOSS WEST, died 13 January, 1802, aged 25.

    JOHN GOSS WEST, died 15 April, 1806, aged 37.

    ELIZABETH, wife of above CHARLES WEST, died 31 July, 1806, aged 67.

    SAMUEL CULME WEST, died 17 November, 1824, aged 51

4. Rev. WILLIAM CLEMENTS, M.A., formerly of Magdalen College, Oxford; Vicar of South Brent, co. Somerset; Librarian of Sion College, London; died 8 April, 1799, aged 88

5. *Crest*—A sangliers head erased in pale [gu] langued [arg] armed [or] for *Whichcott*.

    Arms—Erm. 2 sangliers trippant in pale [gu] for *Whichcott* of co. Linc., impaling — a lion rampant — for ————

    JEREMY WHICHCOTT, Merchant, died 26 February, 1710

    ELIZABETH, his wife, died 26 May, 1733

    Stone laid 1736 by their only surviving child Mrs. SARAH WHICHCOTE.

6. *Arms*—Erm. on a canton [arg] a chevron [gu] for *Middleton*, on an inescutcheon [gu] 3 wheels [arg] 2 and 1 for *Speke* or *Strate*.

    RICHARD MIDDLETON, Senr., died 8 July, 1750, aged 77

RICHARD MIDDLETON, Junr., M.A., his son, died
9 December, 1748, aged 26.

7. Mrs. MARY WILSON, widow of ———— HAYWARD,
and wife of Rev. THOMAS WILSON, D D.,
Rector of the parish, died 4 November, 1772,
aged 79.

THOMAS WILSON, above, died 15 April, 1784,
aged 80.

8   TAMZINE, wife of JOHN DESCHAMPS, Merchant, died
13 March, 1754, aged 38.

JOHN DESCHAMPS, died 28 February, 1776, aged 58.

THOMAS PETER DESCHAMPS, grandson of above,
died 28 May, 1781, in his 5th year.

JOHN, died 12 February, 1847, aged 73.

9. *Crest*—A wing [arg] over it on a pallet [sa] three
crescents of the first.

Arms—Quarterly 1 and 4 [arg] on a pale [sa] 3
crescents of the field for *Hayward* of Norfolk ;
2 and 3 — 2 bars —— in chief 3 buckles —
tongues fess wise points to the dexter for —

JOSEPH HAYWARD, merchant, died — December,
1739, aged 52, eldest son Mr. Deputy SAMUEL
HAYWARD, merchant, deceased, late of the parish
of St Bennet Sherehog.

10. *Arms*—[Arg] 2 chevronels [gu] each charged with a
mullet of 6 points — for *Mower* of Devonshire
on an inescutcheon a hand couped at the wrist
appaumee.

Sir SAMUEL MOYER, Bart, lived in the parish 40
years, died 27 April, 1716, buried 7 May.

Dame REBECCA MOYER, his wife, died 28 January,
1727, aged 77, buried 12 February.

11. *Crest*—A goat's or antelope's head erased.

Arms—an acorn—a chief—impaling—a cross engrailed—between 4—for —

WILLIAM CARTER, of St Bennett Sherehog, died
20 August, 1727, aged 54.

RALPH SHARPLES, his nephew, died 30 November,
1736, in his 37th year.

12. *Arms*— ——————————impaling [Ar] a grey-
hound trippant [sa] collared [vert] rimmed of
1st, for *Morton* of Cheshire.

ABRAHAM BAZIN, only remaining child of five, and
son of GERMAIN BAZIN, merchant, of London,
and ALICE, his wife, daughter of WILLIAM
MORTON, of Chester, merchant, died 2— April,
1693, aged 20.

GERMAIN BAZIN, above, of the parish, born 23
September, 1636, died 28 February, 1704.

ALICE BAZIN, *alias* STRANG, mother of ABRAHAM
above, died 30 March, 1725, aged 82.

13. GEORGE FORDYCE MAVOR, son of Rev. WILLIAM
MAVOR, LL.D., Rector of Bladen-cum-Wood-
stock, co. Oxon., and ANNE, his first wife, deceased died 31 January, 1824, aged 34.

14. DAVID JOHN ALBERT DUVELUZ, son of DAVID
DUVELUZ, Merchant, died 27 January, 1774, aged 5.

JOHN ALBERT DUVELUZ, died 3 August, 1775, aged
15 days.

Miss LOUISA DUVELUZ, died 2 May, 1778, in her
5th year.

SARAH DUVELUZ, wife of DAVID DUVELUZ above,
died 19 March, 1781, aged 37.

15. JANE, wife of RICHARD PRIME, died 4 April, 1797,
aged 56.

RICHARD PRIME, died 1 June, 1804, aged 75.

Mrs. MARY AIREY PRIME, died 28 August, 1835,
aged 68.

16. RICHARD WRIGHT, Merchant, died 17 May, 1748,
aged 62.

EDWARD WRIGHT, his son, died 18 March, 1737,
aged 25.

RENE TAHOURDIN, who married the daughter of
above RICHARD WRIGHT, died 1 March, 1750,
aged 35

Mrs. MARY SMALL, late wife of JOHN SMALL, of
Clapham, co. Surrey, daughter of RICHARD
WRIGHT and relict of RENE TAHOURDIN, died
14 April, 1755, aged 36.

17.   *Crest*—A cubit arm couped, quarterly [arg and sa]
      holding a fleur-de-lis [per pale arg and sa] for
      Nelson.

      Arms—Per pale arg. and sa a chevron between 3
      fleur-de-lis [all counterchanged] for *Nelson*, of
      Yorkshire and London.

      DANIEL HARVEY NELSON, of Loddon, co Norfolk,
      died 23 April, 1760, aged 23.

18   PETER DESCHAMPS, Merchant, died 18 February,
      1757, aged 74.

      CATHERINE, his first wife, died 7 July, 1726, aged 40
      PETER DESCHAMPS, his eldest son, died 10 April,
      1770, aged 55.

19.   *Crest*—A [dog's ?] head erased ——

      Arms— — a chevron — between 3 [dog's ?] heads
      erased ——, impaling. [Sa] a chevron erm,
      between 3 female heads [arg], coupled at the
      shoulders, with hair dishevelled [or] for *Estfeld.*

      REV. NATHANIEL HOOLE, of Wanstead, co Essex,
      died 2 July, 1737, aged 37.

      THOMAS HOUGHTON HOOLE, only son of above, and
      LAETITIA, his wife, died 18 July, 1750, aged 21.

      EDWARD BARROW, late husband of said LAETITIA,
      died 9 January, 1741, aged 29

      LAETITIA, above, died 17 November, 1750, aged 52.

20.   *Crest*—[A lynx arg gorged with 2 bars, or] for
      Langdon.

      Arms—[Arg] a chevron between 3 bears' heads,
      [sa.] for *Langdon*, of Keverell, co. Cornwall,
      impaling Az. a lion pass guardant, or, a chief
      erminois, for *Kent*, of cos. Lincoln and
      Wilts.

      MARY KENT, daughter of DANIEL KENT, and grand-
      daughter of DIXEY KENT, formerly of the
      parish, Linen Draper, died 15 March, 1772,
      aged 44.

      ELIZABETH KENT, sister of MARY above, died
      — February, 1788, aged 57

JANE LANGDON, wife of Admiral LANGDON, sister of MARY and ELIZABETH above, died 30 December, 1805, aged 75.

WILLIAM LANGDON, Rear Admiral of the White, husband of last, died — June, 1785, aged 73.

JOHN KENT, brother of above ladies.

21   *Crest*—A hawk with wings expanded (arg.) for *Bell.*

Arms—(Sa) 3 bells 2 and 1 (arg.) for *Bell* of Bucks and Berks, impaling — on a bend — between 2 escallops — a (martlet ?) — between 2 cinquefoils — on a chief — a rose — between 2 fleur de lis — for ———.

JOHN BELL, died 19 August, 1751, aged 67.

JOYCE BELL, his wife, died 26 October, 1767, aged 75.

ANN CRONKSHAW, wife of Rev. JOHN CRONKSHAW, daughter of above, died 24 April, 1777, aged 60.

22.   GEORGE GRIFFIN STONESTREET, died 24 August, 1802, aged 57, Director of the Phœnix and Pelican Fire Offices.

23.   *Crest*—A raven close (sa.) in his beak a trefoil (slipped vert.) for *Rolfe.*

Arms—(Arg.) 3 ravens sa. 2 and 1 for *Rolfe* of Hackney and Deptford impaling — a cross —.

ANN, daughter of JOHN RAYNSFORD, draper, wife of JOHN ROLFE, skinner, of the parish, died 28 February, 1712, in her 70th year, after forty years married life with said JOHN.

24.   ANN, wife of WILLIAM DICKINSON, many years merchant of the parish, died 1 May, 1787, aged 53.

WILLIAM DICKINSON, above, died 18 April, 1791, aged 54.

26.   ALEXANDER RUSSELL, M.D., died 28 November, 1768, aged 54.

MARY RUSSELL, his wife, died 30 August, 1790, aged 72.

Rev. GEORGE CROLY, LL D., Rector of the parish, died 24 November, 1860.

H

27. MARTHA TOWNLEY, only child of Rev. G. S. TOWN-
        LEY, Rector of the parish, born 1 September,
        1779, died 7 January, 1796.
    Mrs. MARTHA TOWNLEY, died 28 January, 1824
    Rev. G. S. TOWNLEY, died 14 February, 1835,
        aged 88
28. " Mr. STREET's Vault."

All the foregoing are believed to have been formerly in
the floor of the church and removed to the exterior about the
year 1888.

ST. SWITHIN

Ground in Oxford Court.

Headstone

1   NATHANIEL THORNTON, formerly of Lisbon, late of
        Brussels, Merchant, died 4 November, 1839,
        aged 56.

TEMPLE CHURCH

Ground about the Church.

Mural monument

1. SAMUEL MEAD, died 13 April, 1733, aged 63

Pavemental monument.

2   OLIVER GOLDSMITH, born 10 November, 1728, died
        4 April, 1774.

Flat stones.

3. GEORGE HARCOURT, died ————
4   JOHN WYNE, of Inner Temple, died ————
5. THOMAS NASH, of a Worcestershire Family
6. SARAH MARIA BEARCROFT, wife of EDWARD
        BEARCROFT, Barrister, of Inner Temple, and
        youngest daughter of Hon. WALTER MOULS-
        WORTH, died 2— August, 1759

7 SIR THOMAS CLARK, Knight, died 10 November, 1660.

DAME MARY, his wife, died — December, 1675

8 JOHN CHURCHILL died ————

9 ———— son of JOHN GRYMES, of Virginia in America, died 30 June, 1740, aged 22

10 WILLIAM TROLLOPE, Member of Middle Temple, died — 30 March, 1802, aged 69.

11 EDWARD, eldest son of SIR THOMAS LITTLETON, Bart.

INDEX OF SURNAMES

Including those Christian names which appear to be surnames of persons other than, but related to, those commemorated The Christian names indexed are printed in the Index in italics

    The Index numerals against some of the page references indicate the number of times the name occurs on the same page in respect of different monuments

---

Surnames not legible :—3, 6^2, 8, 11^2, 12, 15, 22, 34^2, 36, 43, 56^2, 65, 67, 72, 86^2, 89, 91, 92

INDEX OF PLACES.

HERALDIC INDEX.

Lightning Source UK Ltd.
Milton Keynes UK
UKHW020702090223
416722UK00005B/476

9 780530 670744